OVERCOMING
FLOCCINAUCINIHILIPILIFICATION

OVERCOMING
(FLOX-in-OX-in-ai-hil-i-pil-i-fic-ay-shun)

FLOCCINA

UCCINIHI

ICATION

LIPILIF

VALUING AND MONETIZING PRODUCTS AND SERVICES

JON MANNING

ACKNOWLEDGMENTS

A customer asked a service provider to do a job for them. The job only took two minutes, but when the customer asked "How much?", the service provider replied with an eye-wateringly high price. "But it only took you two minutes to do that!" replied the customer. "No, it took me twenty-five years to learn how to do that in two minutes," replied the service provider.

I've lost count of the number of times I've heard variations of that anecdote, with the service provider being anyone from Pablo Picasso to a lawyer, an accountant and a website designer, just to name just a few.

The same anecdote can be applied to the writing of this book. While much of this book has been written during one of the world's strictest COVID-19 lockdowns, the reality is this book has been a career in the making.

Over the years, many clients and their customers, employers, and workshop attendees have indirectly contributed to the writing of this book. They are too numerous to thank individually. But a number of people have, more recently, provided direct contributions to this book, for which I am grateful:

- **Dr Marcus Powe,** who has been a great supporter of many things I've done, whether it be starting PricingProphets.com or, as readers can tell by the back cover, writing this book
- **Grant Downie,** who for the last seven years or so has allowed me to fine-tune the value-based pricing canvas you will learn about in this book with participants in the Start-Up Leadership accelerator course he runs

- Two of my favorite clients and friends, **Adrian Parsons,** for allowing me to use the Wafex case study in Chapter 22,and **Monique Conheady** for contributing to, correcting, and allowing me to use the Flo Car Share (Flexicar) case study in Chapter 25
- **Chris Grannell** who generously gave his time and feedback on early drafts of this book
- and last but not least, **Lorna Hendry**, for virtually editing and designing and getting the manuscript into the form you see before you today.

Jon Manning
Melbourne, Australia
November 2020

CONTENTS

PART I

WHY PRICING MATTERS

CHAPTER 1

INTRODUCTION

floccinaucinihilipilification

pronounced FLOX-in-OX-in-ai-hil-i-pil-i-fic-ay-shun

noun: The action or habit of estimating
something as worthless

I've been looking for the perfect price for 30 years. It doesn't matter whether I've been a pricing manager, a pricing consultant, a workshop facilitator, a keynote speaker, or an entrepreneur, the quest has always been the same.

"What is the perfect price for my product or service?" is a question I would love to be able to answer with laser-guided precision, by finding a price point (or points) combined with a pricing model that maximizes a business's sales and profit.

Unfortunately, the perfect price is just one of many myths about pricing. By the end of the next chapter, after reading about this and other pricing myths, you will realize the only person who can tell you the perfect price for your product is your customer.

This book won't tell you the perfect price for your product or service, but it will give you a framework to help you identify and communicate, from the customer's perspective, the value of your products and services. It will also provide you with four ways to price your product or service on the basis of value. Those methodologies include:

- the price sensitivity meter
- customer value analysis
- economic value analysis
- subscriptions.

ARE YOU PRICING LIKE DENNIS DENUTO?

I've been involved in pricing goods and services professionally for around 30 years now. I've been fortunate enough to gain experience in dozens of different countries. Along the way, I've experimented with a wide variety of pricing models in a range of industries. My advice has been well-informed with the best of theory and practice, and I'd like to think that it has helped businesses achieve their revenue and profitability goals while maintaining their reputational integrity. But two questions always lurk in the back of my mind: "Did I get the pricing model and the price point(s) right? Could I have made more profit with a different approach to pricing, or higher or lower prices?"

One of my most popular keynote presentations is a talk called "Are you pricing like Dennis Denuto?" – a reference to the bumbling lawyer in the classic Australian comedy movie *The Castle*. Dennis grasps ineptly at whatever facts come to mind, justifying his statements to himself, the judge, and his clients by saying "...it's the vibe, and...no that's it...it's the vibe. I rest my case."

Sadly, this reflects the approach that many businesses take to pricing. The audiences in my presentations often recognize that their past attempts to grab prices out of thin air that "feel right," often without rhyme or reason, has resulted in, at best, the wrong choice of pricing model, serious underpricing of their products and services, or both, and at worst, floccinaucinihilification.

This book outlines a framework I have been using and refining for many years in my quest to develop a sustainable, customer-centric and value-based approach to pricing. That framework is the Value-Based Pricing Canvas.

WHAT IS THE VALUE-BASED PRICING CANVAS?

Readers may be familiar with the Business Model Canvas, a popular framework first proposed by Alexander Osterwalder in 2005 and used by many entrepreneurs and start-up businesses, as well as mature and disrupted businesses, to create or fine-tune their business models.

A new business model is created when new sources of value creation (products) are combined with new ways of monetization (pricing models). The Business Model Canvas helps to define such new business models.

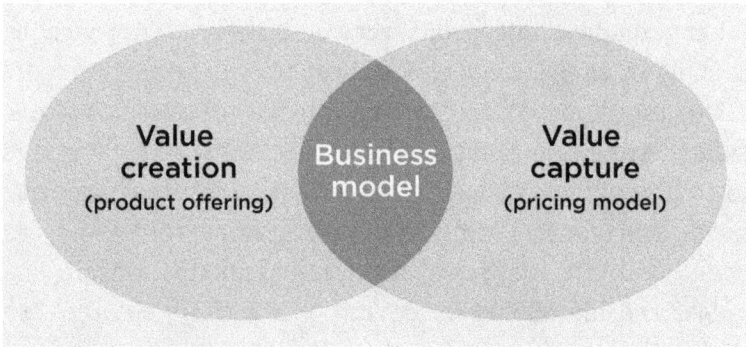

A business model includes value creation and value capture

The Business Model Canvas has nine building blocks, one of which is the revenue streams of the business. The other building blocks are key partners, key activities, key resources, cost structure, value proposition, customer relationships, channels, and customer segments. Given the importance of pricing to the success of a business, the mystery that surrounds it, and the Dennis Denuto–style approach that businesses often adopt, a single building block doesn't seem to do justice to the importance of developing the right pricing strategy.

For that reason, I developed the Value-Based Pricing Canvas: a 15-step framework that will help you recognize the value in a new or legacy product, service, or business model. This also makes it easier to use one of the four value-based pricing methodologies outlined in the second half of the book.

HOW MUCH DOES PRICING MATTER?

Phil is a leadership coach to executive-level managers. When Phil started his consulting career 10 years ago, he was prepared to work 20 days a month. He looked at what his competitors were charging and decided that pricing his services at about 10% below them should help him pick up customers and realize his goal.

Phil soon found himself in a very interesting situation. Firstly, he wasn't attracting the upmarket clients he really wanted to work with. Secondly, the clients he was attracting were asking him to do more and more work for less and less reward.

Phil sought help with his pricing, which resulted in the development of three leadership coaching packages for his clients. The results were immediate. Some of the packages appealed to the upmarket clients that had, to date, been elusive. Other packages clearly defined what services the clients would receive and put an end to the scope creep he had been experiencing. Not only did Phil's clients know what they were getting in each package, Phil knew what services he should be delivering. And, perhaps most importantly, Phil's revenue and profit increased dramatically.

Phil's experience illustrates the power of pricing. This

has been well documented. In their seminal 1992 *Harvard Business Review* paper, "Managing Profit, Gaining Price," Marn and Rosario showed that a 1% improvement in pricing would result in an 11.1% improvement in operating profit. This compares to a 1% improvement in variable cost, sales volumes and fixed cost, which typically result in a 7.8%, 3.3%, and 2.3% improvement in operating profit, respectively.

More recently, McKinsey & Company found that, across approximately 1,000 mid-size firms (US$100 million – US$1 billon in 2017), a 1% improvement in price translates to a 6% improvement in profits.

HOW MUCH WOULD YOU PAY FOR AN ICE-COLD BEER?

In his 2015 book, *Misbehaving: The Making of Behavioral Economics*, behavioral economist Richard Thaler discusses his famous 1985 "beer on the beach" experiment. Thaler asked people what they would be prepared to pay for an ice-cold beer purchased at a five-star hotel at one end of a beach, compared to the same beer purchased from a run-down grocery store at the other end of the beach. He discovered that respondents were prepared to pay a significantly higher price for the beer purchased from the five-star hotel.

Traditional economics assumes human beings are rational. The price they are willing to pay for the ice-cold beer in the two scenarios above shouldn't change. This doesn't explain Thaler's findings.

But behavioral economics can. People act irrationally. Because the context in which their purchase decision was being made changed, so too did their willingness to pay.

Not only is pricing powerful, it is also more art than science. If pricing was a science, we would be able to accurately predict how much a Damien Hirst artwork would sell for at auction. Human behavior and decision-making is both irrational and unpredictable.

WHO IS THIS BOOK FOR?

Over the years, I've observed an interesting trend in workshop attendees from larger organizations: typically, 80–100% of them work in companies that have a procurement department. Yet only 10–20% of these organizations have a pricing department or function. Most organizations are more concerned about the price they pay for products or services they buy than they are in the price they charge for the products or services they sell.

Given that pricing is such an important driver of business profitability and success, why don't companies pay more attention to it?

One reason might be that pricing sits in the "too hard" basket. After all, as Mark Ritson says in Tony Cram's book *Smarter Pricing: How to Capture More Value in your Market*, "Pricing is the worst managed of all marketing areas. How prices are decided is often a mixture of voodoo and bingo." So why invest any resources in it at all?

This book is for entrepreneurs, side-hustlers and small business owners who have heard about the importance of pricing as a profitability driver but haven't really known where to start. The approach outlined here is systematic, customer-centric, and value-based. It will help you solve two key issues about your pricing:

1. how to identify and communicate the value that supports your pricing strategy
2. how to price your product or service on that basis of that value.

HOW IS THIS BOOK ORGANIZED?

Naturally, I would like readers to absorb the book in the way I've written it, from beginning to end. But for those who would prefer to dive into areas of particular interest, here are the options:

- Chapters 2–3: myths of pricing; brief catalog of alternative pricing models, strategies and tactics
- Chapters 4–19: the Value-Based Pricing Canvas and its 15 steps
- Chapters 20–24: value-based pricing methodologies.

Although this book can't tell you the perfect price for your product or service, it will give you a framework for getting as close as possible to it. Hopefully, this will help you avoid floccinaucinihilipilification, and some common and costly mistakes along the way.

CHAPTER 2

PRICING MYTHS

There is no such thing
as the perfect price.

No consultant, software package or book (even this one) can tell you the "perfect price" for your product or service. There's a good reason for this: the perfect price differs from customer to customer, from time to time and from location to location. The existence of a one-size-fits-all perfect price is just one of many myths that surround pricing.

THE MYTH OF FULL PRICE

One of the standout observations in Mark Ellwood's excellent 2013 book *Bargain Fever: How to Shop in a Discounted World* is "How do you make money when full price is no longer guaranteed?"

People not only love the "thrill of the chase" (finding a heavily discounted product), they also love the "thrill of the kill" (actually buying the product at that heavily discounted price), which gives them bragging rights.

Very few people pay full price (or rack rate) for a product or service. To paraphrase Rory Sutherland in his 2019 book *Alchemy: The Surprising Power of Ideas that Don't Make Sense*, "You don't get a dopamine rush from paying full price."

Pricing is a negotiation not a surrender, which means – now, more than ever – that discounting needs to be an integral and strategically managed component of a pricing strategy.

STEALTH PRICE INCREASES ARE A THING OF THE PAST

It wasn't too long ago that price changes were pretty easy. As long as the increase wasn't more than the prevailing rate of inflation, a price change didn't appear on the customer's radar. Today, it's another story. In 2011, when Netflix tried to quietly separate their DVD rental and streaming subscriptions, the *Mercury News* reported that:

> "The comments section on Netflix's own blog entry about its price change hit the maximum of 5,000 posts. On Netflix's Facebook page, members posted 53,000 – and counting – responses. And on Twitter, "Dear Netflix" emerged as one of the top trending topics."

What's worse than a 53,000-customer backlash? How about a public relations disaster than unfolds on a home page of the *New York Times*? Daraprim is a drug used to treat toxoplasmosis, which is an infection that is particularly dangerous to people with weakened immune systems, such as those with AIDS and some cancers. In 2015, Turing Pharmaceuticals raised the price of Daraprim from US$13.50 per pill to US$750 per pill – an increase of 5,500%.

People are also now just as sensitive to a change in size as they are to a change in price. Companies used to get away with reducing the size of, for example, a bottle of tonic water from 315 ml to 300 ml, or the number

New York Times home page, September 20, 2015

of chocolate biscuits in a pack from 11 to 10, without changing the price. These initiatives used to be known as "stealth price increases," but little is stealth-like in the age of social media.

Nowadays, a business has to accept that any changes in their prices have the potential to become newsworthy, conveyed by mainstream and social media to both their customers and competitors.

This means that price changes should be defensible and justifiable on the basis of value. And the bigger the price change, the better the justification that will be required.

A WORLD-FIRST PRICING MODEL

When you've spent most of your career in pricing, it is not uncommon to hear companies or commentators claim that a business has a "world-first pricing model." The reality, however, is often "what's old is new again."

Uber's "surge pricing" is one example. Surge pricing is not very different to the revenue management and dynamic pricing that US airlines introduced after the deregulation of their industry in the 1970s.

If we go back even further, during the Great Fire of London in 1666, boatmen on the Thames doubled and tripled their fares to transport Londoners across the Thames to the safety of the south bank. Grandstand seating at public hangings also increased and decreased according to the level of public interest in the execution.

MARKETS, MECHANISMS, AND THE INVISIBLE HAND

There is no shortage of journalists, economists, authors and businesses (just to name a few) who make statements like, "It's the market that sets the price" or "Prices are set by the invisible hand." In fact, if you subscribe to the school of thought that pricing is decided by a mixture of voodoo and bingo, it would be both logical and convenient to blame "the market" or "the invisible hand."

You only have to get seven pages into Thomas Piketty's *Capital in the Twenty-First Century* to read that "The problem is that the price system knows neither limits nor morality." There may indeed be no limits or morality to pricing changes by the likes of Turing Pharmaceuticals.

But in the overwhelming majority of cases, prices are not set by "markets," "systems," or "the invisible hand." People set prices. You set your business's prices, and you need to take ownership of those prices, as if your business and its reputation depend on it (which it does).

People write the algorithms that trigger Uber's surge pricing. The Thames boatmen themselves doubled or tripled their prices during the Great Fire of London, not a "system" or a "mechanism." And it is your salespeople who get "beaten up" by a procurement manager and end up freely giving pricing concessions or discounts.

OWN YOUR PRICING: GIVE IT A BRAND

We've all heard about "corporate branding" and "personal branding." One way to take ownership of your prices is to give them their own brand.

Apple could have easily branded their iTunes pricing "Why not?" pricing. You hear a song on the radio that you really want on your iPhone/iPod. It's only $1.99. Why not buy it? Supermarkets from Walmart to Tesco and Asda commonly adopt the generic branding of EDLP or Everyday Low Pricing.

There are more advantages than disadvantages to giving your pricing its own brand.

What are the benefits to a professional services company (let's call them "Smith Accountants") branding their pricing Smith's Value Pricing?

By branding your pricing with your corporate name (something that users of EDLP don't do), you make it unique. You've just differentiated yourself with something the competition can never match (unless they acquire you). You are internally and externally stating that you have ownership of your pricing.

For this strategy to be successful, your pricing has to be truly different from the competition. No more picking up an industry benchmarking report and charging the going rate, or something a few percentage points above or below the competition, just to keep the status quo. Leave it for others to tackle customers' perceptions of "sameness" and "commoditization."

As a result of the change (assuming Smith's Value Pricing involves a shift from time-based pricing to pricing on the basis of value), it is likely that some sort of company-wide cultural change program will be required. This provides closure to the old pricing model or approach, and excitement and belief around the new pricing model. That sort of change has to be supported by the upper echelons of the organization: a corporate pricing champion is mandatory.

Last, but definitely not least, this new approach to pricing has to be built into the corporate induction program so all new employees understand how and why the business prices this way. This, along with the pricing champion and the cultural change, embeds the new approach to pricing in the business.

Branding your pricing is not going to be without its challenges. In a professional services firm (legal or accounting, for example), some staff will be early adopters, while others will take a bit longer. Some may never master it. Some people will have trouble having value conversations with customers, when they've been used to having price-based (and discounting) conversations with them. And they will need to think about pricing on outputs and deliverables, rather than inputs.

A variation of this article first appeared on LeadingCompany.com.au on 28 February 2013.

OTHER PROBLEMS WITH TRADITIONAL ECONOMICS

The misuse of economics in pricing goes well beyond the realm of "systems," "mechanisms," and "invisible hands."

How often do we hear about "rising inflationary pressure in the economy," which always seems to be explained away with references to the money supply or the bond market? Just like purchasing managers, who are regularly asked about upstream and downstream manufacturing activity (via Purchasing Manager Indices), wouldn't the right people to ask about inflationary pressures be pricing managers? They are the ones setting the prices of products and services.

And then there are the microeconomic tools of demand and supply analysis and price elasticity. The former is a tool that is so simple that it could be dangerous.

Demand and supply analysis assumes that transactions take place between a buyer and a seller. It tends to ignore the role of intermediaries and the behavior they drive in terms of commercial transactions and demand, never mind being unhelpful in explaining modern business platforms like Uber and Airbnb.

It assumes a company sells a single product, when in fact most companies today sell hundreds, sometimes thousands of products. In 2008, Starbucks took out full page advertisements in US newspapers stating that it offered 87,000 possible drinks.

Finally, demand and supply curves often assume a linear relationship between price and demand. But companies that flex their pricing muscle know that different customers at different times in different markets don't always exhibit linear responses to price changes.

And then there are "Veblen" or "Giffen" goods – luxury or non-luxury goods (respectively) that experience an increase in demand in response to an increase in price.

As for price elasticity, this is a bit like the abominable snowman: everyone has heard about it, but no one is really sure if they have seen it or not. What they often do see are elasticity calculations aggregated across multiple products and customers segments, based on historical data, which don't necessarily take into account advertising or competitive activity, or have relevancy for sales into the future.

PRICING MODELS ARE FOR LIFE, NOT JUST FOR CHRISTMAS

Most (marketing) students are taught about the product life cycle, where a product goes through four distinct phases: infancy, growth, maturity, and decline. It is a myth to assume your pricing model does not go through a similar journey, or that it doesn't warrant similar life-cycle management.

For years, airlines purchased very expensive engines from companies like Rolls Royce, General Electric and Pratt & Whitney. These days, engines are leased to airlines on "power by the hour" contracts. This is effectively a subscription model, the pros and cons of which are discussed in Chapter 24.

BUT THE PRICING MODEL WORKED IN THE SPREADSHEET...

All pricing models work in a spreadsheet. You put the price in Cell B3, the volumes you're going to sell in Cell C3, and the resulting revenue outcome (B3 x C3) magically appears in Cell D3. And the bigger the number in Cell D3, the more excited people get.

There are two simple things to remember about spreadsheet modeling:
1. The assumptions in the model are more important than the calculations.
2. The customer is the single point of failure, and they may not behave in accordance with your spreadsheet formulas.

THE NATURAL FRENEMY OF PRICING IS PROCUREMENT

"Frenemy" is a portmanteau: procurement can be both a "friend" and an "enemy" of pricing. Procurement or purchasing departments are often recognized as the natural enemy of pricing. There is no doubt that they can be a force to be feared, but only for the unprepared.

More companies have procurement departments than pricing departments. It shouldn't be too hard to find a procurement professional who will share with you the strategies they employ to extract lower prices out of suppliers. Armed with this knowledge, you can work out how you're going to counteract those strategies, and ensure you get the best possible price for your product or service.

THE PITBULL VS THE PEACEKEEPER: HOW TO DEAL WITH PROCUREMENT MANAGERS, GWYNETH PALTROW–STYLE

In the 1998 movie *Sliding Doors*, two plots play out between the leads, Gwyneth Paltrow and John Hannah, depending on whether or not Gwyneth's character caught a London Underground train.

Imagine, for a minute, that you are negotiating a huge contract that is worth millions of dollars. You're minutes away from the biggest deal your company has ever signed.

But then something unexpected happens. The head of procurement at the company you're negotiating with suddenly enters the room and tells you they need another 10% cost saving from you or the deal is off.

Just like the plot of *Sliding Doors*, what happens next could go one of two ways.

The head of procurement might play the Pitbull. She starts shouting and bullying, which is part of her sledgehammer approach to an adversarial negotiation to this single transaction. She wants to "screw you into the ground" and take all of that 10% cost saving and rob you of any profit you might make on this deal. To her, profit isn't good: it's dysfunctional behavior. She insists on open-book costing to mercilessly drive down your costs. Your pricing, according to her, is cost-plus or time and materials (labor plus materials, overheads, and margin). She doesn't want to bear any unnecessary overhead costs and probes you on what your overhead allocation methodology is so she can get a cheaper price.

Faced with this approach, what do you do? Three things are probably certain:

- You are going to try and hide more costs.
- You're not going to put your best people on this project.
- You're certainly going to lose interest in the customer who is looking for further cost savings.

But imagine what might happen if the Peacekeeper took control. The scene might play out this way instead: A collaborative workshop is proposed with the objective of finding and sharing a 10% cost saving, which allows you to continue making a profit. Both parties agree to put their best people on the project. The profit incentive remains, and margins remain healthy, resulting in predictable behavior by both parties. The relationship is open and transparent. As both parties work through the open-book costing exercise, cost-reduction opportunities that can be shared are identified. This relationship-based approach focuses on total cost of ownership and lifetime customer value, and the teams recognize that there are alternatives to cost-plus or time and materials pricing, such as guaranteed maximum pricing.

Without a doubt, the movie has a better ending for all concerned in the second scenario.

A variation of this article first appeared on LeadingCompany.com.au on 30 October 2012.

COST-PLUS PRICING IS FINANCIALLY PRUDENT AND RESPONSIBLE

A client once told me that it was financially prudent to use cost-plus pricing, and that any other approach to pricing would be financially irresponsible. He argued you must cover your costs (which is true) and that customers have to (and will) buy products priced on a cost-plus basis (which is false).

While cost-plus pricing is formulaic to apply and simple to explain to customers, it has countless disadvantages:

- It ignores demand, which in some cases can be treated as a proxy for customer value.
- The costs allocated to a particular product, and/or the cost-plus pricing formula itself, may be flawed (try asking an accountant if he know exactly how much of all costs can be attributed to a product).
- You run the risk of over-pricing in weak markets and underpricing in strong markets.
- You end up managing historical expenses rather than future prices and profits.
- It implies that if your costs decline as sales volumes increase, you should drop prices.
- Finally, cost-plus pricing is rather inward-looking, and there is a tendency to either ignore the competition or take it into account as an afterthought.

If levels of demand are not a proxy for value, other sources of value are also ignored by cost-plus pricing. No one selects a certain telecommunications provider or buys a strong, skinny, extra-frothy, caramel drizzle, extra-hot cappuccino from a café because of a business's cost base. They purchase those products because of the value they provide – the network's coverage or the barista's ability to make such a ridiculous coffee.

And of course, cost-plus pricing isn't just a problem in manufacturing industries, where tangible goods are made. It also works its way into services pricing under the guise of time-based billing, or the billable hour.

Cost-plus pricing is also the starting point for our journey around a range of different pricing methodologies, discussed in Chapter 3.

CHAPTER 3

PRICING METHODOLOGIES

Every pricing strategy or tactic has one
single point of failure: the customer.

Chapter 2 concluded with a discussion of the merits of a pricing methodology steeped in the origins of accounting – cost-plus pricing. Although this is a very popular pricing methodology, it is just one of many. Eleven other pricing methodologies are shown in the graphic below.

There are two important things to note about this graphic. The first is that the methodologies are organized into four groups:

- Methodologies 1–4 are pricing methodologies where the pricing is primarily developed by the company selling the product or service.
- Methodologies 5–6 are pricing methodologies where the pricing is often co-created with the customer.

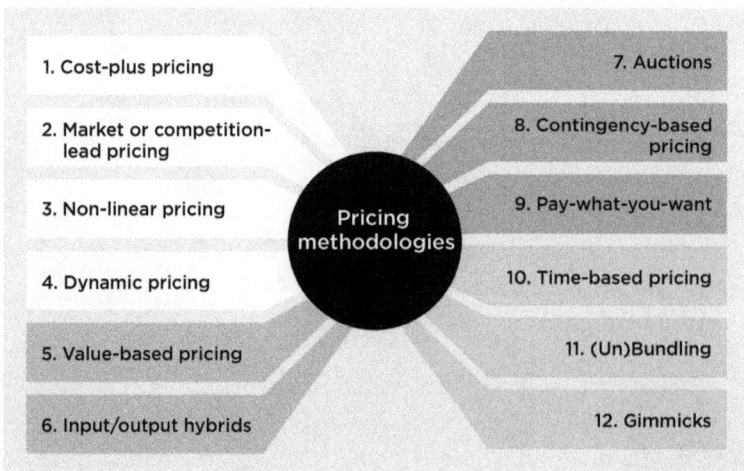

	Pricing methodologies	
1. Cost-plus pricing		7. Auctions
2. Market or competition-lead pricing		8. Contingency-based pricing
3. Non-linear pricing		9. Pay-what-you-want
4. Dynamic pricing		10. Time-based pricing
5. Value-based pricing		11. (Un)Bundling
6. Input/output hybrids		12. Gimmicks

Pricing methodologies

- Methodologies 7–9 are pricing methodologies where the pricing is primarily created by the customer.
- Methodologies 10–12 are commonly used pricing tactics.

The other important consideration is that, while methodologies 1–9 are commonly used as a pricing strategy to achieve a desired long-term goal or outcome, and methodologies 10–12 are commonly used to achieve a specific short-term result, the differences are not always black and white.

Strategy is the approach that a business takes to achieve a long-term goal. Tactics are the specific actions that the business takes in a shorter time frame. Time-based pricing, for example, can be used tactically by a retailer ("50% off, for a limited time only"), but more strategically by a cinema chain ("Half-price Tuesdays").

STRATEGIES 1–4: COMPANY-DEVELOPED PRICING STRATEGIES

There are four methodologies where pricing is (generally) developed by the business for its customers.

Methodology 1: Cost-plus pricing

As its name suggests, cost-plus pricing involves working out the costs to manufacture a good or the cost to provide a service, and then adding on a mark-up, typically the desired profit margin.

This option is favored by accountants as a relatively simple way of pricing that ensures items are priced profitably. That in itself is a huge leap of faith, given the methodology's numerous disadvantages:

- It ignores demand.
- It ignores the value customers place on the product.
- It ignores the competition.
- Calculations of costs and mark-ups can be flawed.
- You can end up managing costs rather than managing profits.
- You can end up underpricing in strong markets and over-pricing in weak markets.

Cost-plus pricing has the potential to leave a lot of money on the table.

Methodology 2: Market or competition-lead pricing

Market or competition-lead pricing is where a business prices its products or service at (or very close to) parity with its competitors. This is a bit like outsourcing your pricing to your competition, but pricing is far too important to be managed this way.

As we discussed in Chapter 2, it's a myth that "the market" or "the invisible hand" controls competitive pricing. Yes, you'll always be competitive on price, but price doesn't always drive the purchase decision, and, like cost-plus pricing, you ignore the value the customer places on your products or services.

Methodology 3: Non-linear pricing

Non-linear pricing is an approach to pricing where there is more than one charge to consume a single product. Many utilities use non-linear pricing. For example, there may be a price to be connected to a gas, electricity or telecommunications network, and separate charges for the gas, electricity or calls that go through those networks.

Some advantages of non-linear pricing are:

- It can be structured to incentivize (or disincentivize) usage.
- There are at least two pricing "levers" that you can flex.
- You can create a "lock-in" (for example, a 12-month commitment).

However, non-linear pricing can be complex and difficult to structure, especially for companies where usage data doesn't exist.

Methodology 4: Dynamic pricing

In the 1970s, the US deregulated its airline industry, removing controls over the cost of tickets and the routes flown, as well as allowing new airlines to start flying. Shortly afterwards, one airline spooked Wall Street, who thought a price war had broken out. The reality was that the inventory their cheap fares applied to had been restricted. This was the beginning of a new era of dynamic pricing and revenue management (remember the Thames boatmen mentioned earlier?), which has now been adopted in industries such as hotels, car rentals, cruise liners, and ride-sharing, to name just a few.

Dynamic pricing is great for highly uncertain markets and (along with auctions, discussed below) for discovering the market-clearing price. It works well with revenue management, which is ideal for products that are perishable (i.e. products that can't be stored for selling later), that have limited or scarce capacity, variable demand, little or no incremental costs associated with selling an additional unit, or where there are opportunities to segment the market.

PRICING: ART OR SCIENCE?

The question of whether pricing is an art or a science has occupied the minds of professionals for as long as I've been in the profession, probably longer. I am firmly of the view that pricing is an art, with the caveat that scientific thinking can help inform better artistic (pricing) decisions. Perhaps the best adjective or portmanteau is therefore that pricing is "artific."

The *Oxford English Dictionary* defines science as "a branch of knowledge conducted on objective principles involving the systemized observation of and experiment with phenomena." If pricing was a science, it would have repeatable laws. A test by one "pricing scientist" could be replicated by another "pricing scientist," and repeated tests would lead to identical results. Yet pricing technology vendors (in particular) still advocate that pricing is a science.

The fact is that pricing deals with human behavior, and human behavior is neither repeatable nor predictable. If pricing were a science, we would be able to predict how much an artwork by Damien Hirst or Banksy would sell for at auction, never mind how much a consumer would pay for an airline ticket or a hotel room.

Perhaps one explanation for why the pricing profession continues to debate whether the trade they ply is an art or a science is that there is no common language. Ask 10 pricing professionals for the definition of "dynamic pricing" or "variable pricing" or "fixed pricing" or "hard bundle" or "soft bundle," and you will not get one simple answer, the way a scientist will give you a law of science, or an element from the periodic table.

METHODOLOGIES 5–6: CO-CREATED PRICING STRATEGIES

There are two pricing methodologies where pricing is (generally) co-created with the customers of a business.

Methodology 5: Value-based pricing

Value-based pricing has two variants, both of which will be explored in greater detail later in the book.

1. **Customer value analysis** is a methodology that seeks to price a product or service according to the customer-perceived benefits of a product or service. This approach is great for business-to-consumer (B2C) products and services.
2. **Economic value analysis**, as its name suggests, involves pricing a product or service according to the economic value it provides to the customer. Great in business-to-business markets, economic value is derived from the ability of the product or service to increase customers' revenue, reduce their costs, or minimize their risks.

Methodology 6: Input/output hybrids

The other pricing methodology that falls into this group of co-created pricing models is input/output hybrids. An example is software, which instead of being sold at full price, is sold at a reduced price plus a percentage of the revenue generated or costs saved.

METHODOLOGIES 7–9: CUSTOMER-CREATED PRICING

There are three pricing methodologies where pricing is primarily created by the customers of a business.

Methodology 7: Auctions

Auctions are a great way (along with dynamic pricing) to determine a price in a highly uncertain or highly specialized market, where the value is unclear, when the item has scarcity value, or where a product needs to be sold quickly. While the seller typically provides the auction mechanism, it is the customer that determines the price at which the transaction takes place.

There are a number of different types of auctions:

- **English auctions** (also known as straight, ascending price, or absolute auctions) are when open bids are conducted for a single item, with the price ascending with each bid. The highest bidder is the winner, who then pays the winning bid. An English auction may run for a specified period of time or conclude at the end of bidding. Seller-specified minimum or reserve prices are not uncommon.

- **Dutch auctions** are commonly used for selling fresh flowers in Holland. Open bids are based on descending prices, and the bid price may be applied to multiple units of the same item. The winning bidder pays the winning price. Traditional Dutch flower auctions conclude in 60 seconds.
- **Yankee auctions** can be used to sell multiple units of a product to multiple bidders. This is perhaps best illustrated by an example: If there are three separate units available to be sold, with bids of $60, $55, and $49, a $50 bid will successfully displace the $49 bid. Each new bid doesn't necessarily have to be greater than the previous bid, or the highest bid, as there are multiple units available.
- **Vickery auctions** feature sealed bids. The highest bidder is deemed the winner, but they pay the price of the second-highest bidder. This gets around what is known as the "winner's curse." The second-highest bid is the optimal price for the item, as the highest bid is made to win the auction.
- **Reverse auctions** feature one buyer and many sellers. The sellers are competing to supply products and services to the company holding the auction.

Most auctions are highly dependent on attracting a number of interested purchasers (or sellers, in the case of a reverse auction) at the same time.

Methodology 8: Contingency-based pricing

Contingency-based pricing is an agreement where the price is determined by another event or transaction. Examples include legal fees that are only payable if a case is won or a transaction (for example, the sale of an asset or property) is concluded.

Methodology 9: Pay-what-you-want

Pay-what-you-want is possibly the most extreme example of a customer-created price point. This model has been used very successfully by websites like HumbleBundle. com, where customers can buy a bundle of digital products and pay whatever price they want. The site is a behavioral economics and gamification playground, because if you pay above the current average price, you get an extra two products in the bundle. We'll talk more about this later.

There are other examples of this pricing model. Proving that this pricing option works offline too, Jon Bon Jovi runs three pay-what-you-want restaurants in New Jersey. During the writing of this book, the website IFTTT.com was offering a "optioned" name-your-own-price offering, albeit at three price points they had selected.

IFTTT Pro

Set your price!

Creatives like you inspire us to keep improving the tools you love. Become an IFTTT Pro and build a more connected future.

- Unlimited Applet creation
- Multi-step Applets with queries, conditional logic and multiple actions
- Faster execution for polling and realtime Applets
- Customer support

Your transaction is secure

1. Sign up or Sign in

Email address

jon.sansprix@gmail.com

2. Payment options

Set your price /month

$3.99 $5.99   • $9.99 $

For a limited time, you may set your price for IFTTT Pro and we will honor it indefinitely. All subscriptions are in US$ and renew monthly.

IFTTT.com website

And perhaps most famously, British indie band Radiohead offered its 2007 album *In Rainbows* to fans on a pay-what-you-want basis, including an option to pay nothing, if fans so wished. Guitarist Jonny Greenwood told *Rolling Stone*, "It's fun to make people stop and think for a few seconds and think about what music is worth, and that's just an interesting question to ask people." The album topped the Billboard chart, among others, and although exact unit and revenue numbers are shrouded in secrecy, *NME* reported that the band's publisher suggested:

> The album had been bought 3 million times, including downloads, CDs and the £40 'Discboxes' that were pre-orderable when the original download went live. 1.75 million of those sales were CDs, and 100,000 Discboxes (a cool £4 million in gross revenues from the latter alone). To put it another way: giving *In Rainbow* away didn't make it worthless. In fact, it was worth a lot more to the band than their previous albums when they'd been signed to a record label.

METHODOLOGIES 10–12: PRICING TACTICS

The final pricing methodologies are more tactical.

Methodology 10: Time-based pricing

Many customers have pricing amnesia – as time passes, they forget the price they paid for a product or service. But time can be combined with pricing to create a large range of useful pricing tactics.

For example, many service providers (such as airlines and hotels) use a "Buy now, upsell later" tactic. Allow customers to buy an airfare or hotel room in advance, and prior to them using the service, offer them the opportunity to upgrade to business class or a premium hotel room.

Similarly, customers might be enticed to "Buy now, complement now." One example is an electrical product with an extended warranty. Sometimes, the fat margins on the complementary product may cross-subsidize the wafer-thin margin on the primary product.

"Free today" is an option often used in financial services, such as a six-month interest-free period on a new credit card. Likewise, retailers are known to "run down the clock" by offering a discount on televisions, but only until the day before the Olympic Games (or another televised event) starts.

As mentioned earlier, pricing strategies and tactics aren't necessarily mutually exclusive. Dynamic pricing also facilitates time-based pricing, whether it is airline seats being sold at different prices at different times of the day, or cheaper early-bird or presale tickets to a performance or conference.

Methodology 11: (Un)Bundling

Bundling and unbundling are two other commonly used pricing tactics. Bundling usually involves selling two or more products at a price cheaper than the sum of the individual prices. Where all the products are available separately, the bundle is known as a "soft bundle." Where one or more of the products is only available as part of the bundle, it is known as a "hard bundle."

Telecommunication companies have made great use of bundling for telecommunications services such as landlines, mobile telephony, internet, and pay-TV services.

However, in other industries, there has been a push

toward unbundling. Apple's music store can be viewed as unbundling the recorded music formats that preceded it, such as the CD and vinyl record (remember them?). Customers can now purchase single songs, rather than entire albums.

Another industry associated with the unbundling movement is low-cost airlines, who have unbundled airfares and now charge separately for components that were previously included in the ticket price, such as baggage and catering. At some airlines, these ancillary revenue streams now account for around 20% of revenue.

Methodology 12: Gimmicks

Gimmicks are the use of pricing tactics to leverage some useful public relations.

In March 2006, the Ostfriesland Hotel in northwest Germany introduced a new pricing scheme where guests were charged 5c per kg per night. Double rooms were priced on the combined weight of the guests, with prices capped at 78 kg in a single room, or 74 kg per person in a double. Traditional hotel room pricing was also available.

In 2019, Alaska Airlines offered fares from the US and Canada to Hawaii where the bigger the forecast surf swell, the greater the discount was.

CONCLUSION

As I mentioned at the start of this chapter, nothing is black and white in the world of pricing methodologies, strategic or tactical. Some readers may argue I've omitted time-based pricing (the "billable hour"), but I would argue that this is a variant of cost-plus pricing. Customers don't care how long something takes to get done, just as they don't care about a company's cost base.

Others may think I've overlooked subscriptions as a pricing strategy. Subscriptions get a chapter of their own later in this book, and they are often, in effect, a non-linear, two-part pricing model, especially those with a variable pricing metric.

What customers care about most, and so should you, is value. In the remainder of the first half of the book, you will learn how to identify the value you provide to customers. We will then come back to some of these pricing methodologies in the second half of the book.

CHAPTER 4

VALUE-BASED PRICING

Q: Where can I find out which features
our customers value?

A: It's in Alvin's head.

As I mentioned in the introduction, the Business Model Canvas is widely used by entrepreneurs and small business owners all over the world. It is a valuable tool, but only one of its steps deals with revenue (never mind pricing!). Given the necessity and mystery surrounding pricing and revenue models, this seemed to me to be a problem that needed to be solved.

The Value-Based Pricing Canvas is my solution to that problem. It is a series of tools and questions designed to help you formulate a picture of the value your product or service provides. Once you understand the value you provide, you can price that value using one of the four methodologies in the second half of this book.

WHY VALUE-BASED PRICING?

In the previous chapter, I briefly mentioned two value-based pricing methodologies: customer value analysis and economic value analysis. What I didn't spend a lot of time talking about is "Why value-based pricing?"

Value is the outcome a customer gets from buying a product or service. That makes it important to the customer, and for that reason it should be important to the company selling the product or service. After all, the customer is the single point of failure: if they don't see value and they don't buy, you don't have a business.

It is also important to focus on value because both the customer and the vendor want to maximize it. Customers typically want to minimize the price they pay, while sellers want to maximize it, so price is a point of friction. However, customers also want as much value as possible, and sellers (usually) want to deliver as much of it as they can.

Price is also an indicator of quality. When it comes to an evolutionary or a revolutionary product, for which customers may have no reference price (a pre-conceived notion of what the price should be), a cheap price will be associated with low quality, while a high price will be associated with high quality.

Customers don't care about your costs, your budget or your six-minute blocks of time. When was the last time you selected a vendor because you liked their cost base, or you accepted a price increase because the vendor wasn't hitting their stretch budget?

Value-based pricing aligns customer and seller interests through co-creation (as discussed in Chapter 3). If you can't communicate the value of your product or service to your customer, you'll either have to resort to selling on price, or your customers will go to a competitor who can communicate their value to them.

COVID-19 AND THE DEATH OF COST-PLUS PRICING

There has never been a better reason to ditch cost-plus pricing than the COVID-19 health and economic crisis that took a stranglehold on the population and businesses from March 2020, and even earlier in other parts of the world.

Cost-plus pricing is traditionally defined as a pricing methodology where you add up all your costs, add a desired profit margin to the sum of those costs, then cross your fingers and pray that customers will pay the price you've just set.

Once set, subsequent adjustments to cost-plus prices tend to be made because of increases in the price of the costs involved (materials, labor, etc.). Lazy businesses may increase prices in response to the rate of inflation (the Consumer Price Index or CPI). The ultra-lazy will just blend this exercise into the annual budgeting exercise their business undertakes prior to the start of a new financial year.

Cost-plus pricing is a sub-optimal method of setting prices at the best of times, but in the worst of times (like during a pandemic), it is utterly useless.

Cost-plus pricing is an impossible task in times of crises for many reasons. The examples given below are based on what was happening among the 90% of Australian companies still actively trading on 30 March 2020, but no doubt these trends will be equally applicable in the future.

- Fifty per cent of Australian businesses have made changes to their workforce, mainly a reduction in the hours that their staff work. Labor costs in a cost-plus pricing model need to be adjusted to reflect this and/or allow for government support payments, perhaps for six months, perhaps longer or shorter ... who knows?
- Thirty-eight per cent of businesses are changing their methods of delivery. For some businesses,

delivery will be a new service they offer, and
therefore a new cost. For others, it may mean more
costs associated with existing delivery options or,
with the recent fall in oil prices, it may mean less
costs ... who knows?

- Thirty-eight per cent of Australian businesses
have renegotiated their property rental or lease
arrangements. The cost associated with the roof
over your head will be changing one way or another,
maybe for the next six months, maybe longer ...
who knows?
- Twenty-nine per cent of Australian businesses are
reporting difficulty sourcing raw materials. Your
output may be using higher priced raw materials,
if you've managed to source them from elsewhere.
If not, your output may be declining, and you don't
know if you should raise prices to reflect scarcity or
drop prices to maintain some cash flow.
- Twenty-four per cent of Australian businesses have
deferred loan repayments. These loans could be
for a range of investments you've made in your
business (such as materials, vehicles, technology),
but whatever you've spent the funds on, deferrals
will have an impact on your cost base.

In a nutshell, the foundation upon which cost-
plus pricing is built has now crumbled. It is useless.
Dangerous. Finished. Kaput!

In the 1860s, Le Bon Marché department store in
Paris ended the era of price haggling and welcomed
in the era of fixed pricing by introducing consumers
to the price tag.

If businesses today want to survive, they will have

to stop using the fixed prices on price tags that are calculated on a cost-plus basis. They will need to talk to their customers, understand the value their products and services provide to them, and price as closely as possible to what their customers are willing to pay, utilizing value-based pricing methodologies.

A version of this article first appeared on the PricingProphets.com blog on 13 April 2020.

OVERVIEW OF THE VALUE-BASED PRICING CANVAS

The Value-Based Pricing Canvas is a 15-step framework designed to help you identify the value of your product or service. It is firmly rooted in a combination of traditional and behavioral economics, complemented with sound commercial, marketing, and management thinking.

Not only does the canvas provide a basis for value-based pricing, it will also help you present that value and pricing to customers in ways that they will readily accept, freeing you from a dependence on selling on price and competitive comparisons.

We will examine each step in the framework in detail in subsequent chapters, but for now I will provide a brief overview of the canvas. You can download a PDF of the full canvas from www.pricingprophets.com/books.

VALUE-BASED PRICING CANVAS

1. The problem	2. Pricing principles	3. Pricing behaviors
What problem are you trying to solve?	What principles do you want to adopt with your pricing strategy?	What behaviors do you want to encourage in customers?
4. Pricing processes	**5. Fears**	**6. Benefits**
What processes do you want to adopt with your pricing strategy?	What concerns might customers have about buying from you?	What benefits might customers get from buying from you?
7. Your appetite for change	**8. Your appetite for risk**	**9. Product value hierarchy**
Low, medium, or high?	Conservative, calculated, or aggressive?	Features, benefits, and value
10. Your economic value	**11. Your value proposition**	**12. Your customers**
Increase in revenue, reduction in costs, and minimization of risk	Value provided, magnitude, and superiority	Scrooge, Goldilocks, or James Bond?
13. Product characteristics	**14. Your competition**	**15. Behavioral economics hacks**
Necessity or discretionary? Unique or commodity?	How do you compete on value and price?	Status quo bias, loss aversion, time discounting, the bandwagon effect, and more

1. **The problem:** This step helps you develop a clear understanding of the specific problem you are trying to solve or address with your pricing.
2. **Pricing principles:** This step looks at the principles you want to apply or adopt around your pricing.
3. **Pricing behaviors:** Pricing drives more than just the behavior to buy or not buy a product or service. This step explores what other behaviors can be driven by your pricing.
4. **Pricing processes:** Pricing is not a set-and-forget project. It is an ongoing process. This step gets you thinking about what processes you may want to put in place to stay on top of your pricing.
5. **Fears:** This step explores the fears your customers may have about buying from you.
6. **Benefits:** This step identifies benefits that will hopefully alleviate the fears identified previously.
7. **Your appetite for change:** Working your way through the value-based canvas may lead you to conclude you need to change your pricing or your pricing model. This step helps you assess your appetite for change.
8. **Your appetite for risk:** Sometimes working with prices has risks: legal risk, financial risk, reputational risk, to name just three. This step helps you assess your appetite for risk.
9. **Product value hierarchy:** This step helps you identify and understand the features, benefits, and the (frequently intangible) value your product or service delivers to your customers.
10. **Your economic value:** This step focuses on quantifying the economic value customers receive from your products or service – how it increases their revenue, reduces their costs, or minimizes their risks.

11. **Your value proposition:** This step helps you understand the product value hierarchy and the economic value generated. This makes it much easier to craft a compelling value proposition.

12. **Your customers:** What type of customer or customers are you dealing with is the focus of this step.

13. **Product characteristics:** This step explores the different strategies you can apply to discretionary products and commodity products.

14. **Your competition:** This step looks at what your product is competing with.

15. **Behavioral economics hacks:** The final step looks at irrational behavior, the psychology that underlies your customers' thinking and purchase decisions, and what constructive role you can play in that thinking.

After carefully considering each of these 15 steps, you will be in better shape to develop a long-term, sustainable, value-based pricing strategy. Start your value-based pricing journey now.

PART II

VALUE-BASED BASED PRICING CANVAS

CHAPTER 5

THE PROBLEM

Despite beliefs to the contrary, pricing cannot solve all your business problems.

The first step in the Value-Based Pricing Canvas asks a very simple but often overlooked question: "What problem are you trying to solve?"

Despite what some people think, pricing cannot solve all your business problems. Your pricing cannot make you the next Facebook of your industry. It cannot make you the next Uber of your industry, and it cannot make you the next Netflix of your industry. Pricing has certainly contributed to the success of those businesses, but there are other reasons for their success.

By answering this question, you should also get a feel for your overall generic pricing strategy. Do you want to be premium priced (a skimming pricing strategy), do you want to grab a big slice of the market with cheap prices (a penetration pricing strategy), or do you want to be somewhere in-between?

WHAT PROBLEMS CAN PRICING SOLVE?

I was recently contacted by the owners of a business who had a very clearly defined problem that they wanted to solve by overhauling their pricing. Their goal was to achieve one of two outcomes:

1. maximize the value of the company in case an

expansionist US competitor sought to gain a foothold in the Australian market through acquisition

2. lock down the Australian market to such an extent that the US competitor would consider it unattractive.

The company pivoted their pricing strategy to multi-year contracts and pricing for their most lucrative customers, as well as making other products free. Both of these initiatives sought to achieve their desired outcomes.

Here are some other examples:

- You want to achieve as much market share as possible (also known as a "land grab"), or capture customers from your competitors. A penetration pricing strategy, where a combination of low price and low value is attractive to the target market, may be one way to achieve this.

- You want pricing that supports your position at the premium end of the market. Pricing has to be at a premium relative to competitive offerings, aligned to aspirational value (when was the last time you saw a premium brand use cost-plus pricing?), and your prices really shouldn't end in 9s or 99 cents.

- You want to focus on the simplicity of your pricing model, so it will appeal to as broad a customer base as possible. Apple's iTunes pricing can be described as "why not pricing." You hear a song on the radio, and decide you want to buy it so you can listen to it on your phone any time you like. It's only $1.99 in the iTunes store – why not buy it?

- You want to move from a transactional relationship with your customers, which has a tendency to run hot and cold, to an ongoing, value-based relationship. A subscription pricing model is ideal for this purpose.

- You want a deeper relationship with your customers. This might be best facilitated with a bundling or a packaging strategy.

As you can see, these are just a handful of problems that pricing can help to solve. This is why the Value-Based Pricing Canvas starts with this problem-defining discussion.

CHAPTER 6

PRICING PRINCIPLES

You can't haggle with a
vending machine.

Wikipedia defines a principle as:

> "a rule that has to be or usually is to be followed... The principles of such a system are understood by its users as the essential characteristics of the system, or reflecting system's designed purpose, and the effective operation or use of which would be impossible if any one of the principles was to be ignored."

A shorter definition of a principle can be found in the *Oxford English Dictionary*, which states that a principle is "a fundamental truth or law as the basis of reasoning or action."

YOUR FIRST PRICING PRINCIPLE

Hopefully, one of the reasons you are reading this book is because you would like to make value-based pricing a fundamental truth, or a pricing principle, for your business.

However, there are some additional pricing principles you may want to consider:

- You will always quantify the economic value of your product or service, rather than picking a price point that "just feels right."

- You will always offer customers three choices to select from: good/better/best, or small/medium/large. This is also known as "Goldilocks" pricing.
- Another pricing principle might be simple, all-inclusive, or "no hidden extras" pricing.
- Alternatively, in a highly competitive and commoditized industry, you may choose to have a more complex pricing structure, which is difficult for competitors to match.
- You might choose to sell only bundles and packages, or you may sell products and services as individual items only. Or you could offer both on a "pick-and-mix" principle.
- In some subscription businesses, the longer the tenure of the customer, the higher the annual recurring revenue and the cheaper the cost to serve. Under these scenarios, it makes sense to offer pricing that encourages longer tenure (for example, 12, 24, or 36-month prices). This is exactly what the company discussed in Chapter 5 did in the face of an expansionist US company.
- You may adopt a principle around price points or price endings. For example, prices that end in zeroes are commonly associated with quality, while prices that end in nines or 99 cents clearly say, "Hey, I'm cheap, discounted or on sale." When was the last time you saw a Hermes Birken handbag (Google it, guys) for $49,999.99?
- In business-to-business markets, you might apply the principle of pricing your product or service just under the buyer's authorized sign-off limit (if known).

Some of these principles may be outward-looking – principles that customers will see. But some principles may be inward-looking – for internal use only.

For example, you might adopt the principle that your pricing model, like the product itself, has a life cycle, so the pricing will need to change during various stages of the life cycle. Alternatively, you might adopt a principle about the frequency and timing of price reviews – once a year, once a quarter, or even more frequently.

Try to select three or four principles and share them across the business. As other people become involved in pricing decisions (for example, product managers), it can be useful to ask, "Does the recommended pricing adhere to our pricing principles?" And don't forget to revisit them every year or two. Ask yourself, "Am I sticking to my pricing principles, or do I need to revisit them?"

CHAPTER 7

PRICING BEHAVIORS

Low prices are not the only
way to keep customers loyal.

Pricing can be used to encourage or drive certain actions or responses from customers, and it can also be used to change their behavior. When you establish your pricing strategy, it is important to think about the type of behavior that you will potentially drive with your pricing.

CASE STUDY: CUSTOMER RESPONSES TO DYNAMIC PRICING

Between 2000 and 2002, a chain of internet cafes became ubiquitous. They spread across the UK, continental Europe and crossed the Atlantic to New York City. Other than during the wee small hours of the night, when prices were fixed (e.g. six hours of internet access for £1), the stores operated on an occupancy-based dynamic-pricing model, just like an airline. Every user that logged in pushed the price slightly higher for the next visitor to the cafe.

Two of these cafes, one on the Iberian Peninsula and the other in a Benelux country, couldn't provide a starker contrast in customer behavior.

On the Iberian Peninsula, students would rush into the store to log on between 8:45 a.m. and 8:59 a.m. They had figured out that if they logged on before the

fixed overnight pricing switched to dynamic pricing at
9:00 a.m., the price of their internet surfing would be
capped at the cheaper overnight fixed price.

Varying the time of day that the store switched
from fixed to dynamic pricing, rather than always
changing at 9:00 a.m., eradicated the stampede.

However, in the Benelux store, the response to
dynamic occupancy-based pricing was quite different.
Customers shied away from the store because they
didn't know how much an hour of internet access
was going to cost them. When this was replaced with
signage indicating which prices applied during which
hours of the day, occupancy increased.

WHAT BEHAVIORS CAN YOU MODIFY WITH YOUR PRICING?

The behavior of customers in the two examples mentioned
above was unpredictable. Later in this chapter, we will
look at some unpredictable behaviors that should be
discouraged. But there are behaviors that are predictable
and can be encouraged with your pricing.

BEHAVIOR TOWARD EARLY ADOPTERS

For a start-up company, or a company with a new brand
or a new product, there is nothing more critical or more
exciting than your first sale. Suddenly your idea is a real
product or service that a customer is prepared to pay

money for. Early adopters are important. They have the potential to not only provide you with the thrill of your first sales but also to become enthusiastic advocates.

How do you nurture these first sales into advocacy? A common mistake I see is that companies immediately think they need a loyalty program. Nothing could be further from the truth. If anything, companies need a risk–reward program (initiatives such as service level guarantees), rather than points for buying this and that. Loyalty is earned, not given away.

It is common at this point to be unsure about your pricing. So why not call it "beta" or "foundation" pricing? This can be made available to early adopters who agree to give you feedback, case studies, video references or testimonials. Depending on the nature of your product or service, these early adopters may be grandfathered on your beta or foundation pricing for a period of time, maybe even indefinitely.

It is worth keeping in mind that, if you look after these early adopters properly, they might go on to become positive advocates for your business and products.

LOYAL AND LONG-TERM CUSTOMERS

If early adopters provide credibility for your product or service, long-term customer "stickiness" provides stability to your business. Loyalty can exist with any pricing model, but some models (like subscriptions and value-based pricing) encourage it more than others.

Early adopters should be rewarded with risk–reward initiatives, but as customers become longer-term propositions, loyalty should (eventually) be rewarded. It is useful to divide loyalty initiatives into two categories:

1. non-financial initiatives, such as better levels of support, training, knowledge, and information, as well as gamification initiatives, such as points, badges, and status credits
2. financial initiatives that you provide to loyal customers, such as preferential pricing (note that I didn't say "discounted pricing" here).

Revenue and profit-maximizing businesses will explore non-financial initiatives ahead of financial initiatives.

DRIVING THE NETWORK EFFECT

Another behavior you may need to work on is building the "network effect." This is a term that is synonymous with online businesses, but which applies equally to non-digital businesses. Basically, if you are selling something, you need to find prospective buyers (or an audience in the online world).

If only one person owns a fax machine (such as former Australian Prime Minster Gough Whitlam was rumored to do at one time), there is no one else to send a fax to or receive one from. There is no network effect.

New ways to overcome the network effect are emerging all the time. Freemium, where there is a stripped-back version of a more functional paid-for product, is one such example. That's now being combined with what is known as product-led growth strategies, where products like Slack and Zoom magically collect email addresses and work for free long enough to get you hooked before converting you to a paid customer.

PRICING MISTAKES AND BEHAVIOR

At the start of this chapter, I said that sometimes you want to use your pricing to encourage certain types of behavior. Making pricing mistakes is a behavior which unfortunately happens from time to time. If it happens once, that's fine, as long as you learn from your mistake. If it happens twice, that's unforgiveable.

Over the years, there have been some very high-profile pricing mistakes. Remember the CEO of Coca-Cola telling the Brazilian media that they were testing temperature-sensitive vending machines that would automatically increase the price of Coke on a hot day?

Other mistakes came in the early years of the commercialization of the internet, when the definitions of offer and acceptance were still unclear. The Hilton hotels in Tokyo and Osaka once uploaded $2 per night room rates – why wouldn't you book a one-year stay (it's cheaper than living at home), as one lucky customer did.

Just prior to Christmas 2018, Cathay Pacific accidentally sold $23,000 first and business class fares for the price of $1,500 economy class fares. A couple of weeks later, the same mistake was unfortunately repeated again.

CHAPTER 8

PRICING PROCESSES

Pricing is not a project,
it's a process.

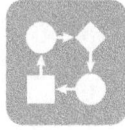

Pricing is not a project, it's a process. And it is good to document some steps in that process, even if it is just a checklist. That's exactly what this step is all about.

Many businesses think a price review is a project that only needs to be done once a year, usually in the lead up to the new financial year (which turns it into a budgeting exercise), or in January to celebrate the new calendar year.

While I support the notion that a product should be scheduled for a price *and* value review at least once a year, the following events are even more important triggers for reviewing your pricing:

- a change in the competitive landscape, such as a competitor entering or leaving the market, new products entering the market...in fact, any change that may affect your market share for better or for worse
- the identification of a new market (either geographical or customer segment) that might warrant a higher, lower or different pricing structure
- a merger or acquisition in your industry that may trigger a change in the competitive landscape – strategic pricing reviews at this point may create an opening for your company that will not be available later on
- a major technological breakthrough that might affect the development, production, or delivery of your product
- a change in your key business processes (for example,

an outsourced supply chain or a function brought in-house) that affects your quality, costs, punctuality of supply or other factors

- a recall or safety warning issued for your products or your competitors' products – proceed with caution in this scenario, as some competitive reactions may be seen as opportunistic and price gouging.

A price and value review is just that: an opportunity to review prices and the value your products provide and check that you are appropriately positioned from both a value and pricing perspective.

You may also find it beneficial to think of your pricing processes as external (communicated to the customer) or internal (back-office).

EXTERNAL PRICING PROCESSES

External or customer-facing pricing processes include:

- **Defining validity dates:** Make sure your prices are "time-boxed" with validity dates that state when they are valid from and when they are valid until. This is particularly important if you are running regular sales and promotions.
- **Developing a pricing calendar or rhythm:** The more products and service you offer, the more price and value reviews you'll need to do. Think about developing a pricing calendar to make sure that, in the absence of any of the special events mentioned above, all your products get some sort of review at least once a year. If your customers buy in advance, they may need to know that new prices aren't available until after this review has been conducted.

- **Conducting win–loss analyses:** Deals aren't always won or lost on price. Conduct a win–loss analysis by contacting a customer after you win or lose a deal to ask why they made the decision they did. Was their decision based on price, product, training, support or something else? If you didn't make the sale, your findings could help you the next time. If you did make the sale, understand what got you over the line. There's always room for improvement.

INTERNAL PRICING PROCESSES

Internal pricing processes, which customers don't necessarily see, include:
- **Establishing discounting authority levels:** Given that discounting is now firmly entrenched into business-to-business and business-to-customer expectations, it might be beneficial to establish who can discount, by how much, and what any escalation processes looks like. Keep in mind that if there are significant increases in prices, either at one point in time or over an extended period of time, these discounting authorizations may need to be revised.
- **Monitoring competitive pricing:** Put in place processes to monitor competitive activity. Just as with win–loss analyses, you may be looking for changes in price or product features as well as additions and deletions to the product ladder.
- **Establishing an evaluation framework:** It is valuable to establish a criteria against which price increases are evaluated. The criteria that have served me well over the years are shown in the table below:

Criteria	Description
Feasible [Mandatory]	The proposed pricing and/or product ladder/feature changes must be feasible from an IT perspective. This is an entry-level requirement, or a "show-stopper."
Value-based [Mandatory]	All recommendations should be value-based and simple for customers to understand in order to gain their acceptance. Aligning perceived value with the price paid is more defensible than a money grab.
Financial return [Mandatory]	Quantify the financial return/revenue uplift from the price changes. Sometimes revenue-neutral price changes are acceptable, but rarely should price changes be revenue-diluting.
Keep the peace [Preferable]	Fine-tuning pricing may be preferable to wielding a sledgehammer. You may need "credits in the bank" to implement changes in the future.
Competitive positioning [Preferable]	If you're offensive against Competitor #1 and defensive against Competitor #2, establish a position from which to tackle Competitor #2, while holding or consolidating your position against Competitor #1.

- **Monetizing new sources of value:** When to start charging for new features or sources of value can lead to much discussion and debate in a business. It always seems to be a three-way tussle between the following scenarios:
  1. monetizing ahead of time, i.e. before the new product or feature is in the customer's hands
  2. monetizing when the new feature becomes available
  3. monetizing after the new feature has landed, and after the customer has seen the value in the updated product offering.

For the record, my preference is the third option.

- **Establishing a pricing committee or council:** In the absence of dedicated and experienced in-house pricing expertise in your business, a pricing committee or council could be a viable alternative. You won't have trouble finding willing participants – everybody has an opinion on pricing. This could also be beneficial from an external perspective. If your sales team are getting beaten up by procurement or purchasing managers, they can always say "That sort of pricing will need approval from our pricing committee."

- **Documenting your pricing strategy:** Consider having a documented pricing strategy. It doesn't have to be *War and Peace*, it can be just a few paragraphs that outline where your products will be premium-priced or mid-market, how you want to position yourself against key competitors, and what your position is on discounting.

- **Recalibrating customer segmentation:** If you have a large number of customers and you have taken the time to segment them all, consider a process and timelines for recalibrating your segmentation model. The customer can change from one segment to another, and they can do it overnight. When an aging father handed over the reins of a family-owned company to his young, ambitious daughter, they immediately went from the most loyal and price-insensitive customer to one who wanted the cheapest prices for everything.

CHAPTER 9

FEARS

A sale is validation of
your business model.

Years ago, on a stopover at Singapore's Changi Airport, I saw USB memory sticks for the first time. I thought it would be great to carry files around on them, but I didn't know whether to get the 64, 128, or 256 MB version. Should I buy the familiar global brand or the cheaper local competitor I'd never heard of? Would there be instructions on how to use it? Would the instructions be in English? Was there a warranty? Would the warranty be valid in Australia? There were so many questions going around in my head for what is now a ubiquitous product that is virtually given away.

Eventually I handed over S$88 for a 256 MB memory stick. It was only a matter of months before the memory stick I had bought wasn't big enough and prices had dropped astronomically. Buyer's remorse set in very quickly.

The questions I asked myself that day in Changi Airport are the questions that customers ask about your product or service every day. Many of those questions are actually fears. That is why they are considered in step 5 of the Value-Based Pricing Canvas.

Some years ago, when the Value-Based Pricing Canvas was in the early stages of development, I did a workshop with a university that was developing a new online collaboration platform for academics. At the time, the whole online collaboration concept was quite new to everyone. Within 10 minutes, one entire panel of the meeting room wall was covered with post-it notes outlining the fears customers might have about buying from them. As I watched the fears go up, I wondered, "How do I get out of this hole that I've dug for myself?"

Fortunately, once we moved on to the next step of the Value-Based Pricing Canvas, (the benefits of buying from them), the post-it notes filled two wall panels. We were able to address all the potential fears. The process of thinking about what the customers feared helped to strengthen their value proposition and identify features that needed to be included or emphasized.

This story highlights the importance of this step... and of following it with quickly identifying benefits, as outlined in Chapter 10.

YOUR CUSTOMERS' FEARS MATTER

Like value, fears or concerns matter to your customers, so they have to matter to you too. The more effectively you alleviate your customers' concerns and fears, the more easily you will be able to influence their buying decision, or even speed it up.

In the story above, many of the fears the workshop attendees listed revolved around the revolutionary nature of the new product we were trying to price. Addressing these fears effectively is important for any product, but it is particularly important for new brands or innovative products where buyers have no real basis for comparison.

Terrifying as it may seem, it is worth spending some time and attention on this aspect of the canvas for two reasons:

1. Uncovering your customers' fears and concerns will help you address them effectively.
2. When you move on to look at the benefits, seeing how many of these fears are eliminated will provide encouragement.

A PRELIMINARY LIST OF FEARS

This list of fears comes from companies who have undertaken a Value-Based Pricing Canvas exercise. It is not exhaustive, but it will stimulate your thinking as you consider your own product or service.

- Can I trust this seller/vendor? Are they credible?
- Has anyone else purchased from this vendor (social proof)? What was their experience like?
- What if there are teething problem with the product? How do I get support? Do they have a telephone number or a support desk?
- Will it work as intended? Is it fit for my purpose?
- Will I lose my job or attract criticism for buying from this vendor?
- How steep is the learning curve for this product or service, and how much time will I need to devote to getting up to speed?
- Will I be recognized as an advocate/early adopter?
- Is my data or my content safe? What is the disaster recovery plan?
- Does this product comply with all the regulations I need it to comply with?

HOW TO IDENTIFY CUSTOMER FEARS

Besides the prompts provided by this chapter, here are two additional ways to identify customers' potential fears and concerns:

- **Start in-house:** Brainstorm internally before talking to customers and prospects. You need to be able to effectively describe your product or service before others can provide useful feedback on it. If the product or service already exists, do a mystery shop to test the experience. Buying your own products is something everyone should do (as is calling your own customer support number). If you run into problems, your customers probably will too, and that will make them fearful. If the product or service doesn't exist yet, map the processes and touch points and ask what could go wrong, and what impression (or fears) that could create.

- **Ask customers or prospective customers:** Even if your product or service doesn't exist, you can still describe it and gauge customer reaction. If you are talking to existing customers, remember that they are sharing their own experience. It doesn't matter if you agree or disagree.

CHAPTER 10

BENEFITS

Raising or lowering prices does not change the benefits on offer to a customer, only their willingness to purchase those benefits.

Right now, you might be feeling like I did during the workshop for the university mentioned in the previous chapter: as if you are facing a mountainous list of fears that customers might potentially have about buying your product or service.

A mantra I've always lived by is "there are no such things as problems, only solutions." It is time to mitigate all those fears by identifying benefits to offset them.

WHAT ARE SOME POTENTIAL BENEFITS?

Here are some benefits that other businesses have used to counteract fears customers may have about a new product or service:

- It provides greater return on investment (remember to use specific, quantifiable metrics that are meaningful and important to customers).
- It will lead to higher employee productivity.
- It reduces the number of steps to do something, the amount of data to be input or reduces the possibility of errors.
- It is easier to use and has greater user satisfaction.
- It is simpler, faster and better.
- It raises the bar when it comes to implementing best practices.

- It beats the competition on features, specifications, warranty, and support.
- It was built by experts in the field – engineers and the like.
- It has fewer unknown costs.
- It features the latest, future-proof technology, with updates automatically delivered via the cloud.
- It is built for local market conditions and/or is supported locally.
- It features seamless integration with, and links to, related products.
- It has hack-proof security and centralized data management.
- It is a premium product.
- It has links to, or endorsements from, expert associations.

HOW CAN YOU IDENTIFY THE POTENTIAL BENEFITS?

A great place to start identifying the benefits of a new product is with the product manager. They will have had a specific problem, use case, outcome, or job to be done when they conceived and built this product. If the product already exists, your sales and service teams are a great resource for identifying benefits.

If you think about what the product or service is designed to do, you will be able to find specific features, characteristics, or metrics that it improves. These can be listed among your benefits.

Once you have identified as many potential benefits as possible on individual post-it notes, you can line these up against the fears. Hopefully, your list of benefits will immediately cancel out all (or almost all) the fears your customers might experience.

If not, you have some more work to do before you have finished this brainstorming session. Ideally, you will find enough benefits (in strength, if not number) to easily outweigh their fears.

THE IMPORTANCE OF BENEFITS

In addition to alleviating the fears your customers may have, a clear understanding of the benefits your product will deliver will help you:

- create a value proposition that opens doors of opportunity with a hook that is immediately relevant to the customer
- develop marketing collateral that resonates with your buyers and creates opportunities
- optimize the monetization opportunities for your product.

Skilled salespeople open the door for their pitch by starting with something the customer really cares about having or seeing.

CHAPTER 11

YOUR APPETITE
FOR CHANGE

To change prices, point-and-click...
don't rewrite code.

As mentioned in Chapter 2, it wasn't that long ago that price changes could be executed in stealth-like fashion, and noticed by few (if any) customers. Those days are long gone: the internet detects price changes and social media amplifies them.

There will always be unknowns. Customers do not do exactly what you want them to, based on your Excel spreadsheet. In real life, their behavior can be very different. Likewise, you may think competitors will do one thing, but in reality, they could do something completely different.

You need to assess your business's appetite for change. Simplistic words at the extremes of a scale (like high or low, conservative or aggressive) disguise the complexity of this assessment.

Change is a process, and that process requires a plan. The biggest point of failure associated with price or pricing model changes is the execution.

Before drawing up a coordinated plan to execute price or pricing model changes, it's worth giving thought to some preliminary considerations:

- Does this price change signal a change in your positioning in the market?
- Will this price change shift your position relative to your competitors?
- Does this price change apply across the board, or does it only apply to certain products or markets?

- How will this price change affect and be perceived by existing customers?
- What is the purpose of this price change (in terms of principles or behaviors)?
- Are you committed to this price change even if you experience short-term pain?

By thinking through these elements in advance, you will be able to pre-empt some undesirable consequences and (at the very least) be prepared to respond to others quickly and effectively.

For an annual price change, the process detailed in an execution plan may include:

- management time spent evaluating and modeling the magnitude and outcome of the proposed price change
- updating of marketing collateral, rate cards, price list, websites, distributor/wholesaler arrangements, etc.
- sales force training
- updating pricing repositories and/or billing systems.

Pricing model changes are typically always bigger than just dollar and cent changes to price points. Some additional steps for a pricing model change could include:

- a short "dipstick" survey with a very small number of customers to assess how they feel about the proposed pricing model change
- a pricing pilot, where a small number of customers trial the new pricing model
- a staged implementation, with the migration of the least risky customer segment to the new pricing model (mistakes will be less costly), before moving on to the core customer base.

CHAPTER 12

YOUR APPETITE FOR RISK

If you want to win at pricing,
you will have to take some
calculated risks.

While change is a process, risks are associated with the outcome of those changes. And there are risks in every pricing decision.

Two of the biggest risks are:

1. What will your customers do?
2. What will your competitors do?

As comfortable as your modeling may make you feel, the customer is the single point of failure in a purchasing decision. A price change may result in a decision to buy or not buy from you anymore. Price too high and nobody buys. Price too low and you may be swept off your feet with unprofitable levels of demand.

Typically, entrepreneurs have a greater appetite for risk and more courage when it comes to pricing, but you should enter this arena with your eyes open and an understanding of your comfort levels.

If you are an established company that already has products and services in the market, you need to take your appetite for risk into account whether you are launching a new product or changing the prices on an existing one.

Changing prices is not easy. Whether you are increasing or decreasing your prices, you risk losing your customers to your competition.

It would be wonderful if this exercise were risk-free, but it's not. Like anything in business, it is a double-edged sword: get it right, and the rewards are huge; get it wrong, and the downside can be devastating.

Whatever your choice, you need to back yourself and the decision you make.

CHAPTER 13

PRODUCT VALUE HIERARCHY

All value is subjective.

Every product has three unique elements:

1. They have operative **features**, or product specifications. These features enable the product to do what it is meant to do. (As we'll see later in the book, products also have non-operative features).
2. Those product features provide **benefits** to customers.
3. Products deliver **value** to customers (the outcome they get from the product experience).

Features and benefits are primarily objective and can be determined by the vendor of the product or service. Perceptions of value, however, are subjective. They are determined by the customer, although this can be influenced by the vendor.

EXAMPLE: PRIVATE HEALTH INSURANCE

Private health insurance is a great product for illustrating the difference between the features, benefits, and value of a product.

Most private health insurance policies include a range of features such as dentistry, optometry, and physiotherapy. The benefits associated with these features are usually expressed as dollar amounts for the particular types of services, for example, $250 per year of optometry services.

Ask people why they have private health insurance and you'll get a variety of reasons. For some, the value is simply the fact that they don't have to pay the extra costs. For others, the value is the peace of mind it provides. Others value the ability to get out of the public health system and receive care in the private system or choose their own doctors and specialists. And for others, it will be about getting back on the road to recovery (and work) faster.

A CAUTIONARY TALE: REAL ESTATE

Value is subjective and determined by customer perception. Sometimes even putting yourself in your customers' shoes doesn't safeguard you from the unexpected, as the following real-life example will illustrate.

During the 2000s, I was helping a real estate advertising portal monetize the value of the services they sell to real estate agents. Various advertising products (the features) would deliver email leads to agents (benefits) that would enable them to sell a property (and earn their commission) as quickly as possible.

Following the successful launch of its iPhone app, the company decided to introduce click-to-call functionality, and position that functionality to justify some of its latest price increase. The logic, from the company's perspective, was inarguable: a prospect sees a desirable property, clicks the telephone icon, and speaks to the real estate agent who then schedules an appointment.

Given the significance of the product launch and the change in value, I decided I'd go on a "ride-along" with a sale representative. I wanted to hear how they positioned the new source of value, relative to the accompanying price increase. I also wanted to know if our perception of the value of click-to-call leads was aligned with the real estate agent's perception of value.

The agent listened quietly and intently as the sales representative did a great job positioning the new source of value. When asked for feedback, the agent leaned back in his large leather chair, looked at the sales representative, and said, "I don't want click-to-call."

The sales rep was baffled. "Why not?" he asked. "This is the most qualified and accountable lead that any business can possibly give you."

"Yes, I get that. But I don't want people calling me any hour of the day or night just because it suits them. I'm happy with email leads that I can read and respond to when it suits me ... and besides, not every enquiry is a good lead."

This example just goes to show that the seller isn't always the best judge of what the customer will value.

CHAPTER 14

YOUR ECONOMIC VALUE

Charge customers a fraction of the incremental value your product or service generates for them.

In Chapter 13 we looked at the fact that value is subjective and is determined by the customer. Despite this, in business-to-business markets, and to a certain extent business-to-consumer markets, there are three generally irrefutable sources of economic value. We call it "economic value" because it can be quantified to the customer, in economic (or accounting) terms.

ECONOMIC VALUE ANALYSIS

The premise of economic value analysis is that there are three ways to provide value:

1. Your product or service can increase your customers' revenue.
2. Your product or service can reduce your customers' costs.
3. Your product or service can minimize your customers' risks.

Each these three sources of value are economic; therefore, they can be quantified and demonstrated through calculation.

Let's look at some specific examples of sources of economic value.

REVENUE

If a company's product or services increases revenue, this could happen in a number of ways:

- It might provide customers with access to a larger market, so they can attract more customers or change the mix of customers (for example, more premium customers).
- It might allow the customer to charge higher prices because they are able to deliver more value.
- It might result in a manufacturing improvement that enables the company to produce more product, a higher quality product at the same cost, or a similar product with higher profit margins.
- It might help customers get their products and services to market more quickly, reducing the lag between production and revenue.

COST SAVINGS

Your product or service might facilitate cost savings through:

- reductions in labor costs
- reductions in marketing or other costs
- reductions in bad or doubtful debts
- efficiencies, for example, the automation of processes or better handling of materials.

MINIMIZATION OF RISK

Ways that risks can be minimized include:
* ensuring staff are always working with the most up-to-date technology, minimizing staff departures and turnover
* proactively managing compliance issues (workplace, legal, regulatory) resulting in the avoidance of fines and penalties
* protecting customers from cyber or ransomware attacks (online software is particularly useful in this regard).

Economic value analysis will often work in business-to-consumer markets as well. Some products will allow consumers to increase their income, reduce their expenses, or minimize their risk(s).

HOW THIS WORKS IN PRACTICE

One of the first projects conducted on www.PricingProphets. com was on behalf of an entrepreneur from a developing country in which a spate of kidnappings and other occurrences was causing concern for the parents of school children. The entrepreneur had recently launched an SMS text messaging service that advised parents when their child arrived safely at school.

The entrepreneur's intention was to validate the price he was charging the parents of the children. Since there was limited uptake, he wanted to confirm his pricing model. The experts recommended a pricing model he hadn't considered, which was to charge the school a per-student-fee based on a percentage of the school fees (rather than charging the parents).

WHY WAS THIS MODEL SO ATTRACTIVE?

For the entrepreneur, this simplified his sales and marketing tremendously. Instead of having to persuade each parent, he only had to sell his proposal to the school once. The school would then deliver the service to every parent (the schools became a "multiplier"). This greatly reduced the size of his projected sales force. In addition, since his fee was based on a percentage of the school fee, his revenue went up in proportion to the fees without any need on his part to negotiate a price rise with the school.

From the school's perspective, this was also an attractive proposal. Parents were concerned about their children's safety, and the school was able to position itself as caring and responsible for the children entrusted to their care.

CHAPTER 15

YOUR VALUE PROPOSITION

If you can't explain value,
expect the customer to go to
a competitor who can.

All products have an implicit value proposition. The Value-Based Pricing Canvas helps you quantify that value proposition clearly to prospective buyers so you can sensitize customers to value and desensitize them to price.

In the absence of product knowledge, which is often the case for start-ups with evolutionary or revolutionary products and services, price provides an indication of quality.

If the price significantly exceeds the customer's perception of value, the product may be considered a rip off. Conversely, if the value significantly exceeds price, prospective customers may consider the offering too good to be true or think there must be something wrong with it.

The best value propositions tend to tell the reader or listener three things, in a simple and succinct way:

- It tells them what value is provided.
- It quantifies the magnitude of the value provided.
- It explains how the value provided is superior to that of the competition.

WHAT VALUE DOES THE PRODUCT PROVIDE TO CUSTOMERS?

If you've completed the previous step of the Value-Based Pricing Canvas, you'll already know what value your product or service provides.

If that exercise identified a single source of value, your choice is easier than it would be for a product or service that has numerous sources of economic value.

If your product or service has numerous sources of economic value, for the purposes of developing a generic value proposition (for example, for a website or generic marketing collateral) use the source of economic value that is most likely to appeal to the widest possible audience and is the easiest to communicate.

However, for customer-specific sales pitches, it may be beneficial (and possible, using various technology products) to develop different value propositions that align with the interests of the customer. For example, you might have one pitch deck for customers who are more interested in your product increasing their revenue, another for customers who are interested in cost reductions, and a third for customers who are interested in risk minimization.

TO WHAT MAGNITUDE DOES THE PRODUCT PROVIDE VALUE?

Your value proposition should then be embellished by quantifying the value added. Examples include:

- "On average, our product increases customers revenue by 19.6%."
- "The typical customer using our product experiences a 12.7% reduction in labor costs."

You'll notice that the numbers mentioned are very specific. This is because you will have done the numbers and quantified the value delivered. Rounded numbers like 10% or one-quarter may be interpreted as having been made up.

HOW IS THE PRODUCT SUPERIOR TO THAT OF THE COMPETITION?

The final hallmark of a great value proposition is its uniqueness. It needs to be something that you own, and that no direct or indirect competitor can take it from you.

There is a simple test for this. Take your company name out of the value proposition and replace it with that of one of your direct or indirect competitors. If it is possible for that value proposition to work for your competitor, it is not unique. Refine and refine your value proposition until you get it to a point where no competitors can use it.

CHAPTER 16

YOUR CUSTOMERS

"If I have 2,000 passengers and
400 prices, I'm short 1,600 prices."

Robert Crandall, former President and
Chairman of American Airlines

There are many ways to think about segmenting your customers. Segmentation can be done on many levels and it plays a very important role in both your pricing and your marketing.

There is no such thing as the perfect price, but by segmenting your customers and offering different segments of customers different price points, you are more likely to get closer to a perfect price than you will with a "one price fits all" approach.

If you carry that idea to its logical conclusion, isn't customer-specific pricing like nirvana to pricing professionals? Yes and no. There is no doubt that customer-specific pricing is likely to minimize the consumer surplus and maximize revenue. However, if at some point in the future you need to change pricing models, migrating customers from a multitude of different price points to a new pricing structure can be a headache.

SEGMENTATION

Basic demographic and firmographic information has for a long time been a staple of segmentation models. Many businesses seek to identify segments of customers who can be grouped into clusters based on dimensions such as age, gender, marital status, income, profession, etc.

Firmographic segmentation may look at business-related dimensions such as corporate structure, years in business, and number of outlets, just to name a few.

I would probably run out of fingers and toes trying to count the number of companies I have seen build purely descriptive, "warm and fuzzy" segmentation models. The most important feature of an effective segmentation model is that it is *actionable*. That means it can be used to market or advertise to each segment differently, or price to each segment differently. Why segment customers if you can't action the segmentation?

Step 12 of the Value-Based Pricing Canvas involves identifying the pricing personas of your customers. You need to embellish these personas with customer-specific data that is beyond the scope of this book. The following three personas provide a starting framework:

1. **Scrooge:** Named for the penny-pinching character in Charles Dickens' *A Christmas Carol*, these customers are acutely sensitive to price and value. They are the customers that want you to explain why the price of a cup of coffee went from $4.50 to $4.55. They are also the ones who want to know why a bottle goes from holding 315 ml of tonic water one day to 300 ml the next day, without a price change. If your customers lean toward a Scrooge persona, you need to think through any price changes extremely carefully before you present it to them. If you don't have a very persuasive justification, you may lose them.

2. **Goldilocks:** "Not too hot, not too cold, I like my porridge just right!" said Goldilocks, and that's exactly how these buyers think about price and value. To choose the right porridge, they have to understand the value of the alternatives (one is too hot and the other is too cold).

3. **James Bond:** Staying on the literary theme, many people have a touch of James Bond in them, always wanting the best of everything. Apple fans are a good case in point. I've asked hundreds of people in workshops over the years two questions: Are they Apple fans or not, and why? In every case except one, the reply from Apple fans is because it works, because of the functionality, because of the features, because of the brand. Not one person has said they buy Apple products because they are more expensive than competitors. Apple has done a great job of bringing out the James Bond in all its customers: they have sensitized them to value and desensitized them to price.

Continue to build out these pricing personas, for example with estimates of their willingness to pay, the cost to acquire them, and the ongoing cost to retain them.

CHAPTER 17

PRODUCT CHARACTERISTICS

Value is a function of features, benefits, and price. If price exceeds features and benefits, the customer doesn't buy. If features and benefits exceed price, you're leaving money on the table.

Years ago, I stumbled across an article on pricing in *Business Week* magazine that included a two-by-two matrix. The first axis had "Commodity" at one end, and "Unique" at the other. The second axis started with "Necessity" and ended with "Discretionary."

Perhaps more interesting than these two axes is the quadrants they form. The two quadrants on the right-hand side tend to be where premium pricing opportunities reside. The two quadrants on the left-hand side are where pricing needs to be sharper and more competitive.

1. **Discretionary and unique products:** Any business that finds itself in this quadrant should have substantial pricing power and the opportunity to charge premium prices. Most Apple products would fall into this quadrant, as would super-premium vehicles, like the Mercedes-Maybach S-Class Saloon (to name just one).

2. **Necessary commodities:** Nearly every house-branded product would sit in this quadrant. However, some companies with products in this quadrant may seek to take them upmarket, into the next quadrant.

3. **Discretionary commodities:** Commodities can become discretionary. There are many basic toasters on the market with room for two slices of bread and a 1–5 temperature setting. But double the capacity to four slices, make the slots wider to accommodate crumpets, add additional temperature controls, and

all of a sudden you have a "café style" toaster, which – while still being a commodity product – is now a discretionary purchase.

4   **Unique necessities:** The final quadrant is for unique necessities. The toothpaste aisle of any Western supermarket is a shining example of such a product. Years ago, there were two choices in this aisle: Colgate and Macleans. Today, toothpaste is still a necessity, but there are many, many unique variants – whitening, gum protection, fresh breath, etc (even charcoal!).

CHAPTER 18

YOUR COMPETITION

Sophisticated pricing means
more than just working out
what the competition charges.

The penultimate step of the Value-Based Pricing Canvas introduces the competitive environment into your value-based pricing mindset.

Step 14 is a value map (see the example in Chapter 22, p. 142), which is a very useful and pragmatic way to show how companies and products compare with their competitors on price and value. A value map typically shows price on the vertical axis (with price rising from the lowest price at the intersection with the horizontal axis, to highest) and the horizontal axis showing a measure of value.

Like the pricing power matrix in the previous quadrant, the axes on a value map are interesting, but what they reveal is more useful. A value map for the automotive industry would have a lower-price/low-value brand like Kia in the bottom left corner. In the center are mid-price and mid-value brands like Toyota. In the top right are high-priced, high-value brands like BMW or Mercedes-Benz.

A diagonal line drawn from the bottom left to the top right is known as the value equivalence line. The area above the value equivalence line is a not a good place for a business. Any company operating in that space is unlikely to be successful, as it would be selling at higher prices than its competitors, and customers could get the same value for a cheaper price from another company.

But below the value equivalence line is a different

proposition. This is often where disrupters find themselves, offering cheaper prices for the same (or less) value than their competitors.

Value maps are easy to construct for some industries and more difficult for others. In the automotive industry for example, details on product specifications can be used to create the scale on the horizontal axis, while price information (before discounts) is also readily available for the vertical axis. Technology products are also relatively easy to construct as well.

In industries where technical specifications are harder to find or ascertain, and pricing is more overt than covert, value maps may need to rely on significant amounts of personal judgement.

We will look at more value maps in the Part III of this book.

CHAPTER 19

BEHAVIORAL ECONOMICS HACKS

"You don't get a dopamine rush
from a mid-market purchase."

Rory Sutherland, *Alchemy: The Surprising
Power of Ideas that Don't Make Sense*

In Richard Thaler's "Beer on the Beach" experiment, students, picturing themselves sitting on a beach on a hot summer's day were asked how much they were prepared to pay for an ice-cold beer purchased from a five-star hotel compared with one purchased from a run-down grocery store. Traditional economics says there should be no difference in their willingness to pay. It's the same beer – why should there be a difference? Thaler however, found otherwise. There *was* a difference, and traditional economics couldn't explain why.

These findings around irrational behavior have now formed a body of knowledge known as behavioral economics. When used correctly, the learnings can be applied to your pricing.

The following are some of the key discoveries that have been made in the field:

- **The status quo bias:** People are biased toward the existing or default option. As long as it is the option that is in the customer's best interest, they will appreciate the nudge when, for example, the box on that alternative is already checked for them.

- **Loss aversion:** Customers perceive the pain of a loss as approximately twice as potent as the pleasure of a gain. This is why surcharges can discourage certain behavior and discounts can encourage it. Cheap cinema tickets on a Tuesday night will stimulate demand, but a

Saturday night surcharge will stifle it.

- **Time discounting:** People are generally biased more toward rewards in the present than rewards in the future. This principle has important implications for the success or failure of loyalty initiatives. If you can bring the rewards closer to the reach of the customer (for example, by stamping the first two of 10 purchases on a coffee loyalty card), you increase the likelihood that they will buy the other coffees.

- **The bandwagon effect:** Humans are a bit like sheep. They are generally biased toward social norms and the decisions taken by others. Customers are inclined to choose suppliers with a large and growing market share, as they have already been endorsed by others. This is also known as "social proof." Pricing pages on websites often show a "Most popular" badge for this reason.

- **Ambiguity aversion:** People dislike taking risks they cannot accurately quantify. Clear rules, processes and plain English contracts, terms and conditions are just taken for granted.

- **Heuristics:** Many people tend to use a "rule of thumb" to reach a decision rather than making exhaustive calculations. For this reason, it is important to simplify their decisions as much as possible and talk in the language of the customers. If one such rule of thumb is "the average small business spends 2.5% of turnover on a software product," tell the customer what percentage of their turnover your pricing represents.

- **Anchoring:** Different ways of presenting your pricing can result in different responses. In Western countries, people read from left to right, so the first number or price they will see becomes an anchor against which subsequent prices will be seen as either cheaper or more expensive.

- **Overconfidence:** Because people overestimate both the accuracy of their own judgments and their ability to control future behavior, they will often overestimate their demand. Companies can help customers make more informed choices, but they can also help them buy too much (and have to deal with the remorse and ill will that accompanies that).

- **Projection bias:** People assume that what is true this week, year, or month will still be true in the future, even when there are predictable changes that will almost certainly alter those trends.

- **Choice architecture:** Sometimes the easiest road to "Yes, I'll buy it" is to offer three choices. Give a customer one choice and you have a 50:50 chance of closing the deal. Give the customer two choices, and you'll force the majority of customers into making a price-based decision. But give a customer three choices and two things happen:

  1. The customer says, "Which one do I buy?" rather than "Do I buy?".
  2. The customer is forced to make a value-based decision, as they explore the reason for the price differences across all three products.

- **The left-digit effect:** It is common knowledge that most people interpret a $29.99 price point as cheaper than a $30.00 price point – which it is (by $0.01). But the perceived difference is much larger: it's the difference between a price point in the 20s vs a price point in the 30s. Restaurants often drop both the currency symbol and one or more decimal places on the prices on their menu. The objective is to desensitize customers to the fact they are parting with their money.

- **The center-stage effect:** This is when a company puts the product they really want to sell in the middle of the offering – for example, in the center of a menu. If they really want to emphasize it, they might put a fancy box around it as well.
- **Post-purchase rationalization:** Whatever the real reason for a customer purchasing your product or service, as soon as the purchase is complete, there's a chance the customer will attempt to rationalize their decision. This is why it is a very good reason to ask customers for a rating or recommendation, referral or testimonial before the euphoria of the purchase wears off. It is also why people don't return their purchases immediately.
- **The Ikea effect:** Is there any benefit in asking customers to assemble their own flat-pack furniture? It turns out there is. Involving customers in the assembly of a product actually increases the buyer's perception of value. This is a powerful reason for involving your customers in set-up or training.
- **The zero price effect:** Unsurprisingly, demand increases dramatically when the price is zero or free. Conversely, demand for a product that was previously free also falls when customers are asked to pay for it.
- **The sunk cost fallacy:** This describes consumers' attempts to maximize the amortization of an investment as much as possible. Amazon Prime gives subscribers access to digital products and faster deliveries for a modest monthly subscription. On Amazon Prime Day, these subscribers get access to subscriber-only discounted prices. Amazon Prime Day is (in pricing

and behavioral economics circles) commonly known as "sunk cost fallacy day," as Amazon Prime members buy stuff they don't necessarily need or want, just to maximize the return on investment they get from their membership.

- **Colors:** Colors can affect customers and the choices they make in different ways. The table below explains the perceptions of a number of colors.

Yellow	A color commonly associated with optimism and youth. It is also great for grabbing people's attention (e.g. window shopping).
Orange	An aggressive, but positive and inspiring color, which makes it great for calls to action.
Pink	A very romantic and feminine color, with strong appeal to women and young girls.
Green	An easy-to-read color, great for those with a love of nature, which conveys messages of hopefulness, balance and growth.
Red	A color that energises. It raises the heart rate and creates a sense of urgency, so it works well during sales and clearances.
Blue	A color commonly used by banks, for obvious reasons: it is a color associated with trust, security, and honesty.
Purple	A color commonly associated with royalty, regalness, and exclusivity. It is also calming and soothing.
Black	A color commonly used to promote luxury products and services. It is sleek and powerful.

EMBRACING BEHAVIORAL ECONOMICS... OR GAMIFICATION?

Before closing this chapter, and this section of the book, I'd like to share with you an example of a business that embraced behavioral economics (and a bit of gamification) in their business model.

In 2012, HumbleBundle.com offered a bundle of (at the time) five digital products (books, games, etc.).

The offer was only available for a limited amount of time, which created a sense of urgency. The pricing model was a pay-what-you-want model. If anyone paid above the current average price, it unlocked an additional two digital products. Anyone who paid an above-average price helped to drive up the average price the next buyer had to pay to unlock the two extra products.

Pricing model on HumbleBundle.com.website.

The site also allowed buyers to specify how much of their payment they would like to go to the author/creator of the book/digital product, how much they would like to leave to a charity, and how much they would like to go to the HumbleBundle website.

HumbleBundle demonstrated a brilliant use of both gamification and behavioral economics to engage viewers and prompt them to purchase.

I hope this gives you some ideas about different ways that you might be able to slice and dice your prices and the way you present them to increase uptake on your most profitable products and services.

PART III

VALUE-BASED PRICE POINTS

CHAPTER 20

ESTABLISHING VALUE-BASED PRICE POINTS

There's a huge difference between "setting" a price and "getting" a price.

After working through the Value-Based Pricing Canvas, you should now understand the value of your product and be ready to price your product on the basis of the perceived value it delivers to your customers, rather than the costs associated with its creation.

There are four methodologies that do this particularly well. These will be explored in the chapters that follow. They include:

- price sensitivity meter, a methodology which involves talking to customers about their willingness to pay
- customer value analysis, which involves talking to customers about prices and perceptions of value
- economic value analysis, which sets prices on the basis of revenue uplift, cost reductions, and/or risk minimization
- subscriptions, which are currently the pricing model of choice for many products and services.

In case you didn't notice, all four of these approaches to value-based pricing require you to talk to your customers, or prospective customers. You cannot do pricing from an ivory tower or from the comfort of a co-working space, spare room, or garage.

The four methodologies described in this section of the book are abbreviated and can be treated as simplified and agile approaches to price setting. They can certainly be made more elaborate (for example, see *The Joy of Pricing* by Michael Hurwich for a more comprehensive treatment of customer value analysis).

Remember that the more artificial your research, the less realistic your results will be. If you are researching prices with customers, show them the most realistic mock-ups or prototypes of your products or service. If you're researching prices for a service, try showing them website wireframes. And don't hesitiate to introduce competitors and their pricing into the discussion either. It's always easier for customers to provide relative, rather than absolute, feedback on pricing.

Finally, keep in mind that the customers or prospects you are talking to will quickly work out that you are asking them about pricing. If they are seriously interested in your products, their natural tendency may be to lowball their suggested pricing. Pay attention to how you frame the questions you are asking. Instead of asking "What would you pay?" ask "What do you think a company like yours would pay?"

CHAPTER 21

PRICE SENSITIVITY METER

Mistake #1: Overestimating customers' price sensitivity.

Mistake #2: Underestimating customers' willingness to pay.

n 1976, Peter Van Westendorp introduced his price sensitivity meter to the world in his master's thesis. It was adopted quickly because it provides a relatively straightforward, easy-to-calculate method of determining value-based pricing that can be used in both business-to-business and business-to-consumer markets. It is a popular way of gauging willingness to pay.

The price sensitivity meter methodology involves asking customers four price-related questions:

1. At what price does the product look cheap? (Cheap)
2. At what price does the product look expensive enough that you would have to think carefully before purchasing it? (Expensive)
3. At what price does the product look so expensive that you would never consider buying it? (Too expensive)
4. At what price does the product look so cheap that you would feel it couldn't possibly be worth buying? (Too cheap)

The results are then graphed. The answers to two of the questions (1 and 4) are inverted, resulting in a graph that usually has four intersecting lines. A prospective price point lies within the boundaries of these four lines:

• The intersection of the Too Cheap line and the Expensive line is the point of marginal cheapness.
• The intersection of the Too Expensive line and the Cheap line is the point of marginal expensiveness.

Price sensitivity meter output

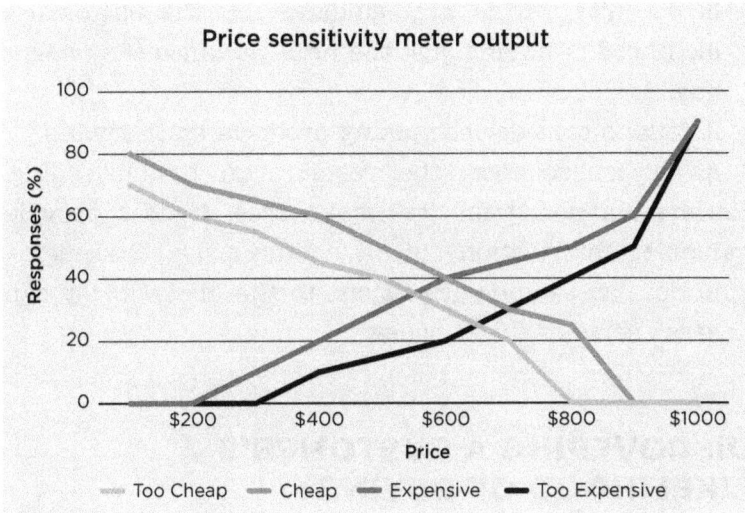

- The intersection of the Expensive line and the Cheap line is the indifference price point.
- The intersection of the Too Cheap line and the Too expensive line is the optimal price point.

As its name suggests, the optimal price point is the price point that maximizes demand for the product or service.

It is important to note the slope of the curve for each of these lines. A steep curve suggests that there is a greater risk of setting the wrong price and losing customers. A shallow curve means there is greater scope to increase prices without losing sales.

DISADVANTAGES OF THIS METHOD

The price sensitivity meter has some significant drawbacks:

- It often identifies a range of prices rather than a single definitive price point.

- It doesn't provide any guidance on the customer's likelihood of buying, just the price at which they might buy.
- It fails to consider competing products and services.

As a consequence, the results can be misleading. However, allowing for its weaknesses, it does provide valuable information in a notoriously challenging situation, and minor alterations to the methodology can address some of these issues.

DISCOVERING A CUSTOMER'S LIKELIHOOD OF BUYING

The biggest drawback of this method is the lack of an objective indication concerning people's likelihood of buying. What people say they will do and what they actually do can be two completely different things. A workaround for this involves asking, "On a scale of 1 to 5, what is the likelihood that you would buy this product at $X?"

Responses to this question would be adjusted, taking 90% of respondents who answered "Definitely," 40% of those who said "Probably," 10% of those who said "May or may not," and the rest of the responses being ignored. (These adjustments are known as the Urban and Hauser scale.)

Alternatively, you could ask the equivalent question, using an 11-point Likert scale, and adjust the results by the Juster scale.

ENHANCING THE PRICE SENSITIVITY METER

In their 2016 book *Monetizing Innovation: How Smart Companies Design the Product Around the Price*, Ramanujam and Tackle abbreviate Van Westendorp's method to three questions:
- What price is acceptable?
- What price is expensive?
- What price is prohibitively expensive?

This yields an arguably even more valuable result, because it is quite specific. You can see an example of price curves generated from this questioning below:

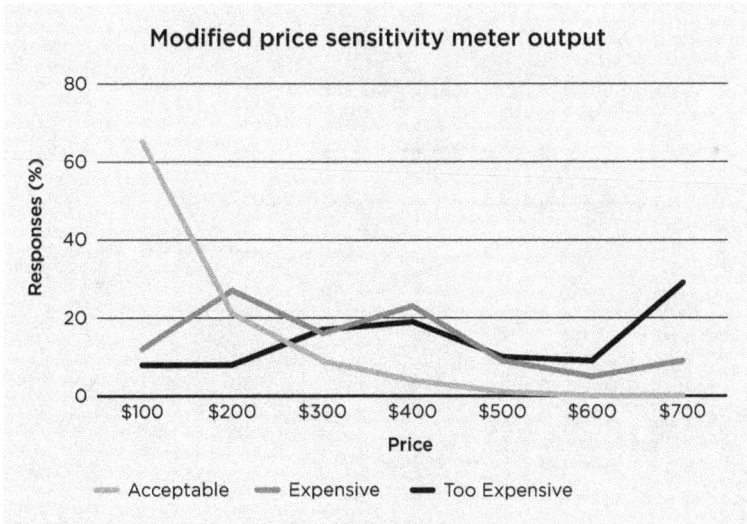

Modified price sensitivity meter output

I recently used this abbreviated version of the price sensitivity meter and drew on the net promotor score concept to evolve it a step further.

Using the three questions above, I subtracted the percentage of respondents that found a price point expensive or too expensive from those who found the price acceptable in order to arrive at what I call the net acceptable price.

This approach yields a series of take-up values (percentages) along a price curve. In the example below, you can see the net acceptable price becomes negative (or unacceptable) just before reaching $200.

The price point with the highest positive net acceptable price (in this case, approximately $100), is the price that should yield the highest level of demand (approximately 45%).

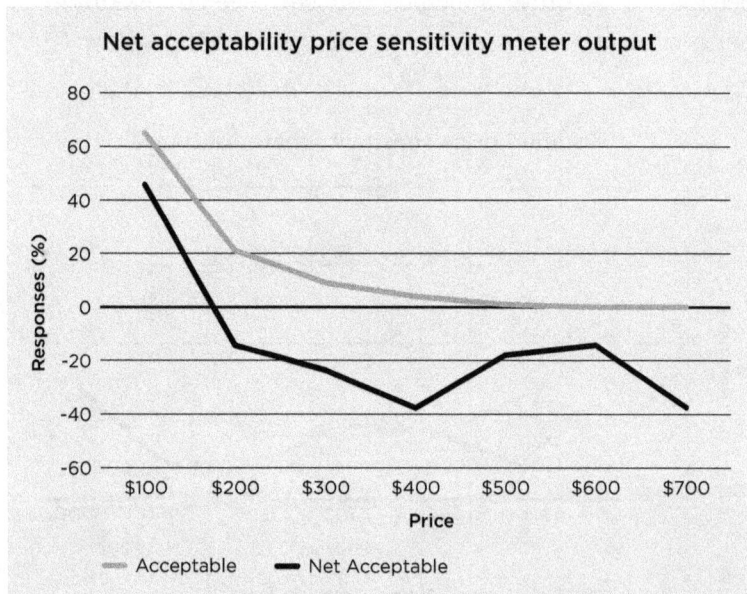

Net acceptability price sensitivity meter output

These examples were adapted from a consulting engagement where we learned that what was thought to be a "one-sided market" (where advertisers paid to reach an audience who used the website for free) was in fact a "two-sided market" (where segments of the audience were also willing to pay).

There are three critical advantages of this methodology:

1. You have to talk to customers to do it, and you should talk to them using the language and findings from your completed Value-Based Pricing Canvas. It is customer-centric and value-based.

2. It demonstrates that pricing research can be cheap, quick, and affordable.

3. You have an opportunity to confirm or reject assumptions about who will pay for products and services and how much they are willing to pay.

ASSUMPTIONS AND CUSTOMER CONVERSATIONS

Two of the three critical advantages involve actually talking to customers. As a behavioral economist, I love testing models and data but, as a pricing expert, I know that these valuable tools have some serious limitations unless they are firmly rooted in the real world and customer results.

One of the advantages that existing companies have over start-ups is the fact that they have customers who can be a mine of valuable information. As illustrated in the example above, they can also shatter well-founded assumptions about who will actually pay for your products and services, as well as what they value.

CHAPTER 22

CUSTOMER VALUE ANALYSIS

All pricing is relative, not absolute.

Customer value analysis aims to quantify the value of a product and its most important features from the customer's perspective.

This helps you discover what specific attributes of a product your customers value most, which allows you to use that information to price and visualize your company's products and services in the context of your other products or services, or your competitors' products.

HOW TO PERFORM A CUSTOMER VALUE ANALYSIS

1. Identify the main value attributes of the product. Ideally you should do this by asking the customers. If this is not possible, you can get acceptable results by asking a product manager or your sales force. I usually aim to identify anywhere between four and six critical value attributes.

2. Ask the customers to weight the critical value attributes. For example, they may weight quality at 25%, brand at 50%, customer service at 15%, and ease of use at 10%. The sum of the weightings should be 100%. This step may need to be conducted across a group of customers before moving to the next step, which really requires the use of group consensus weightings.

3. Decide if you are going to ask customers to rank the product you are trying to price against:
a) another product that you offer (which has already been priced) and/or
b) a competitor's product.
4. Ask customers to score each of the products on the critical value attributes. Use a scale of 0–10 or 0–100.
5. Multiply each customer's score by the weighted ranking for each of the critical value attributes. Your table should look like the example below.
6. Add up all the weighted rankings to arrive at an index number (shown in the "Total" row in the table below). Use this to compare the product you are pricing with the product already offered and/or the competitor's product.

Attributes	Weight	Product being priced		Product already offered		Competitor's product	
		Score	Weighted ranking	Score	Weighted ranking	Score	Weighted ranking
Performance	40%	7.0	2.80	8.0	3.20	5.0	2.00
Battery life	25%	8.0	2.00	7.0	1.75	6.0	1.50
Warranty	25%	9.0	2.25	6.0	1.50	7.0	1.75
Brand	10%	3.0	0.30	2.0	0.20	1.5	0.15
Total/index number	100%		7.4		6.7		5.4
Price				$299		$259	
Comparison using indices				$299 x 7.4/6.7		$259 x 7.4/5.4	
Calculation of price using comparisons				$330		$355	

This methodology can be used to benchmark one product against another, or one company against another, as well as to assess which attributes are most valued by your customers. This is invaluable information for your marketing, too. Collateral and sales pitches can be centered around the critical value attributes that are most important to the customer.

Value map

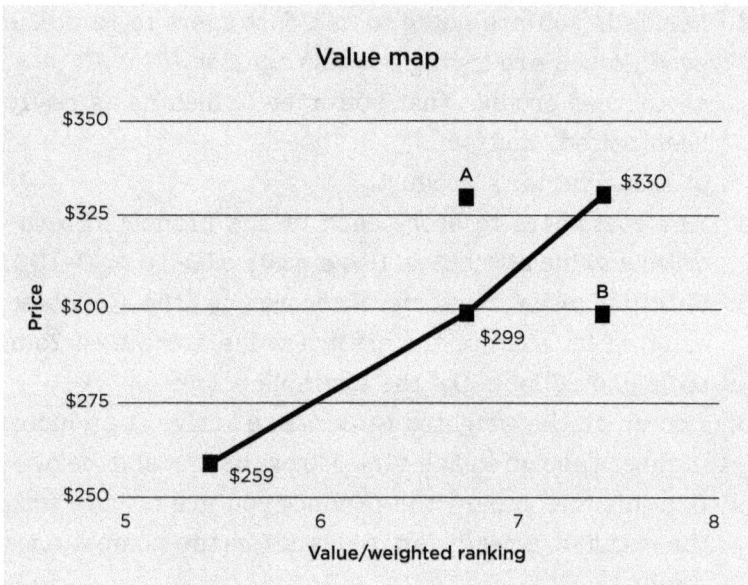

It also gives you a "value map" – an easy-to-read snapshot of where your product fits into the marketplace. In the example above, we can see the price of the competitive offering ($259), the price of a product already priced and offered ($299), and the price we'd charge for the new product if we based it on the product already offered ($330).

If our new product landed around point "A" on the value map, where the price is higher but the value identical to the existing ($299) offering, the product is likely to be unattractive to customers. If the new product landed around point "B" on the value map, this would leave money on the table as the price is the same as the current offering, despite the higher value. (Alternatively, this product could have the potential to disrupt this market.)

LIMITATIONS

This methodology works best when there is a set of established products and competitors and a relatively evenly distributed market share. If a single player has cornered 80% of the market and 20 small players are competing for the other 20%, this methodology is of little use.

Another limitation with customer value analysis is that, while it provides a strategic overview of your competitive situation and allows you to anticipate the impact and anticipated competitive response to proposed strategies, it is more of a historical tool than a forward projection. In a rapidly shifting marketplace, it can lose relevancy very quickly.

Finally, customer value analysis will not provide information about price sensitivity.

CASE STUDY: WAFEX

Wandering around the Melbourne Flower Market at 4:00 a.m. with Wafex co-founder Adrian Parsons, listening to buyers (wholesalers and florists) and sellers (flower growers) openly calling the prices they are haggling about, you realize how price-driven this industry is and how difficult (if not impossible) it would be to change price perceptions or the pricing model in the industry.

Wafex is one of Australia's largest fresh flower wholesalers, with offices in Melbourne and Perth. Adrian, who is highly respected in the industry, has never been one to shy away from business model innovation. The peak season for fresh flowers in Australia starts just before Valentine's Day in February and runs until Mother's Day in early May. It's the time of the year when demand and sales make up for the leaner months during winter. And it was the winter of 2009 when Adrian rang me and said, "Let's see what we can do with pricing during this 'off-peak' winter season."

Using customer value analysis, I spoke to several flower growers (and Wafex customers) about what was most important to them when it came to the wholesalers they deal with. The weighting they assigned to the four most important value attributes mentioned were:

- Range and product: 45.8%
- Service and support: 18.3%
- Convenience: 18.3%
- Price: 17.5%

The flower growers were asked to rank Wafex and its competitors on a scale of 1–10 across these four value attributes. The raw and weighted rankings are shown for Wafex in the first graph on the next page. The raw and weighted rankings for the competitors are shown in the second graph. Wafex was clearly doing a better job with non-price attributes compared to its competitors. Wafex's customers were less sensitive to price than other wholesalers.

Armed with this insight, a range of initiatives were developed and pursued over the winter, including:

- segmentation of customers (groupings of customers who share similar needs, desires, preferences, or characteristics, and price sensitivities)

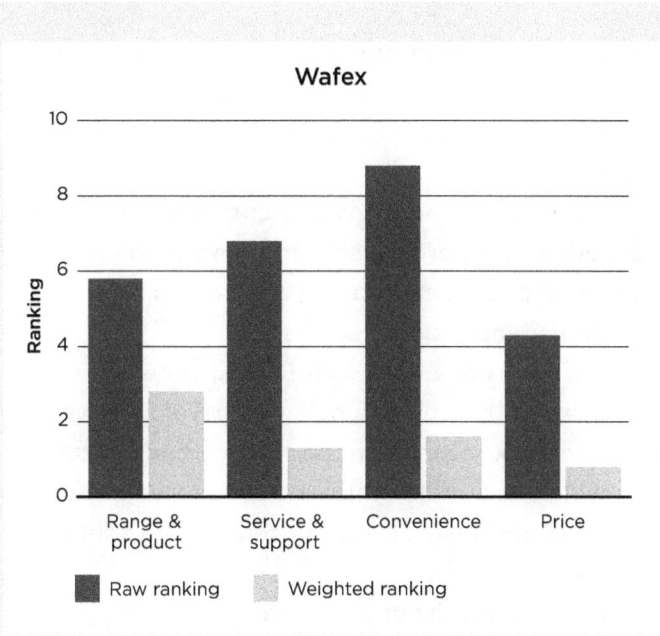

Wafex

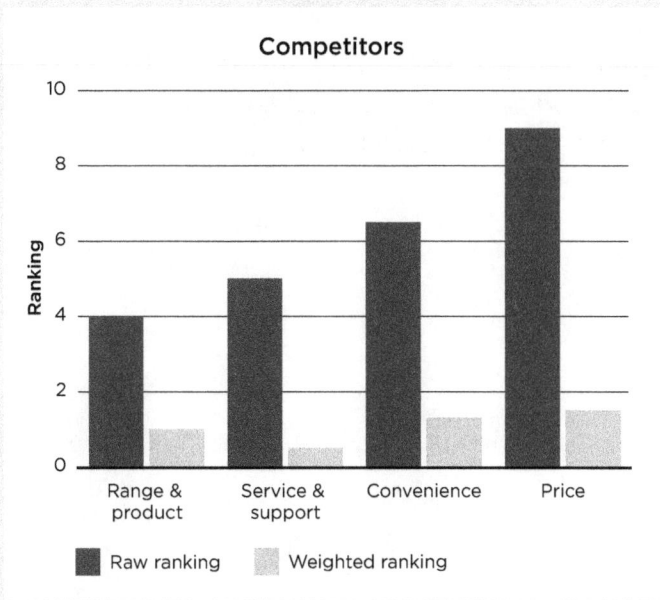

Competitors

- segmentation of products (groupings of products that share similar customers, demand, service similar or complimentary needs and a similar pricing strategy)
- creation of a two-dimensional customer-based and product-based pricing strategy, which covered a different pricing strategy for each combination of customer and product segments.

To manage objections surrounding price increases, particularly for roses, a bundle was developed where customers could maintain their legacy pricing, subject to buying this bundle, which included minimum quantities and Wafex selecting colors and varieties on their behalf.

What were results of this strategy?

- The volume of roses sold increased by 2.5% on the previous winter.
- Turnover increased by 17.1%, thanks to a 14.3% rise in the average price per unit sold.
- Gross profit increased by 6.7%.

CHAPTER 23

ECONOMIC VALUE ANALYSIS

The most important number
in your business is the one on
your price tag.

At the heart of value-based pricing is the notion that sellers or vendors share the economics of a value-creation process with their customers. For example, a software platform that delivers a $1.5 million increase in total economic value (based on increased sales or a higher selling price) could have its prices expressed as 5% of the economic value created (or $75,000).

As we saw in Chapter 14, there are three ways to quantify economic value to the customer and reflect it in your pricing:

1. improving revenue
2. reducing costs
3. minimizing risk.

In any value-based pricing model, but particularly in economic value analysis, a strict adherence to the model implies that the prices of your products or service may also fall, as well as rise, in response to changing economic conditions, competition, or technological developments. A company that truly believes in value-based pricing will not be afraid to decrease prices when value declines, for whatever reason.

The other thing to keep in mind with value-based pricing in general, and economic value analysis in particular, is that it is harder to sell and compete on value than it is to sell and compete on price. However, the rewards are greater, and it certainly takes you out of the race to the bottom, which is often the fate of many price-focused companies.

ECONOMIC VALUE ANALYSIS ISN'T EASY

It is very difficult to be prescriptive about how to do economic value analysis. Every product will provide different sources and magnitudes of economic value against different competitors for different customers.

The table below provides some avenues to explore in the quantification of your economic value.

Category	Benefit	Measurement
Improve revenue	Increase volumes Sell at higher prices/ yield Create new revenue streams Open up new channels Open up new markets	Measure the incremental revenue attributable to the product Measure the total revenue attributable to the product Quantify the size of new revenue streams Measure the benefits on a one-off or on-going basis, as applicable
Reduce costs	Reduce one or more categories of expenditure	Estimate any reductions in cost of goods sold, which may take the form of opening or closing stock, raw material purchases Quantify the value of savings in ordering times Measure any reductions in other expenses

Category	Benefit	Measurement
Minimize risk	Quicker time to market Improved safety and quality Environmental benefits Legal compliance On-time deliveries Improved productivity Innovation, research and development Wastage and replacement Life of the product	Measure "First-Mover" or "First-to-Market" benefit Measure the costs avoided from, for example, litigation or carbon taxes Quantify savings from waste and spoilage reductions, as well as costs of holding replacement parts

IMPROVING REVENUE

For example, if your product improves your customers' revenue, this could be derived from initiatives such as:

- increases in the number of units sold
- existing products sold at higher prices than previously
- opening up new revenue streams, new markets or new channels to market.

Once you have identified how you improve their revenue, quantifying that benefit may involve calculations revolving around:

- measuring the incremental revenue generated from additional units sold or from the slightly higher price
- measuring the total revenue attributable to the product
- estimating the size of the new revenue streams, new markets, or the value of the new channels.

These calculations should also take into account any negatives effects, such as the possibility of cannibalization of existing products in the case where, for example, a cheaper product is introduced to market.

REDUCING COSTS

Similar exercises would have to be performed for products that reduce costs. The natural starting point to quantifying the benefits of cost reductions would be the profit and loss statement (preferably that of the prospective customer):

- Does your product or service change the complexity of cost of goods sold?
- How much does your product reduce marketing expenses?
- How much does your product reduce labor costs?

MINIMIZING RISK

What about risk minimization? Look no further than the example of cloud-based software, which is an intangible product. Unlike software of old, it doesn't come in a fancy shrink-wrapped box with user manuals. Rather, it is sitting there when you open your browser.

The economic value of risk minimization on cloud-based products can be huge:

- Software is always up-to-date and compliant (important in industries such as tax and legal software).
- Staff are always working with the latest software (keeping staff morale and retention high).
- There are reduced or diminished chances of a cyber or ransomware attack as the risk is typically carried by the cloud-based software provider.

When you have quantified the economic value, how do you work out what share of that economic value you capture in your pricing? The answer to that could come from multiple sources:

- traditional market research with customers
- rules of thumb (for example, companies typically pay 1.5% of sales on a software product)
- competitive comparisons, taking into account points of similarity, points of difference, and points of contention compared with competitors
- opportunity costs (Bain and Company calculated that there were more than two million cyberattacks in 2018, which resulted in losses of US$45 million).

COMMUNICATING ECONOMIC VALUE ANALYSIS TO CUSTOMERS

The process of communicating economic value to customers is getting more and more sophisticated. It wasn't too long ago that "value word equations" were popular: give the customer a simple equation that will enable them to compare, for example, a cost saving from using Company A against the cost saving associated with using Company B. If the figure for Company A is greater than that for Company B, the customer would be better with the Company A. If the outcome was the opposite, the Company A would be better off with Company B.

These days, sales representatives are armed with more rigorous value calculators, such as sophisticated Excel spreadsheets or purpose-built apps. These tools help them communicate the value to customers effectively (remember, *all* customers care about value) and show them different usage or use-case scenarios. Furthermore, value can be illustrated to prospective customers well ahead of price, and price objections can be managed by removing items that customers don't value, or adding additional items that they do value, and providing additional flexibility and customization.

In business-to-business markets, where economic value analysis really excels, your product or service may be competing with an in-house solution. Do customers make it themselves or buy from you? By stacking more value into your product, relative to the price you are asking, you're more than likely to encourage the customers to make the decision to buy rather than make.

CHAPTER 24

SUBSCRIPTIONS

"Don't you know these days
you pay for everything."

Bruce Springsteen, "High Hopes"

THE RISE OF SUBSCRIPTIONS

Over the last decade, there has been a huge proliferation in the subscription business model. According to *The Economist*, between 2011 and 2016 the US subscription market is estimated to have expanded from US$57 million in sales to US$2.6 billion. By 2027, it is forecast to reach US$350 billion. Today, there is very little you cannot buy on a subscription, from entertainment to underwear. It's not just a US phenomenon either. In Australia, you can purchase subscriptions to just about everything, from television and music to headphones, coffee, and pet food.

The pricing question you should be asking is "Should I be implementing a subscription model in my business?"

WHAT'S DRIVING THE RISE OF SUBSCRIPTIONS?

There's no denying the fact that (pre-COVID-19) Wall Street was rewarding subscription-based businesses with valuations that were 10 times higher than transactional-based businesses, because it prefers the stability of recurring revenue, especially when that stability is paired with phenomenal growth.

Entrepreneurs and start-ups are also finding that angel investors and venture capitalists are more interested in subscription-based businesses than transaction-based businesses. It's not uncommon to see investors on LinkedIn stating in their profile that they are only interested in businesses that have achieved $500 million in annual recurring revenue.

WHAT'S SO GOOD ABOUT SUBSCRIPTIONS?

Let's start by looking at the benefits of subscriptions for sellers and customers.

For sellers

- They provide predictable revenue streams to the vendor.
- Vendors "sell once, renew many" which, particularly over the long term, can reduce the cost to serve the customer.
- When combined with product-lead growth strategies, there are cost synergies associated with the selling and onboarding processes that reduce staff numbers and manual processing and effort.
- Subscription companies have higher valuations due to the recurring revenue stream.

For customers

- Subscriptions to cloud-based technology provide easy access to upgrades and the latest software.

- Other subscriptions provide instant gratification and availability to music, movies, etc. without the need for storage.
- Subscriptions can provide variety (a different flavor each month) and ensure a product is always available for consumption.
- Subscriptions can provide access to items that are unavailable or hard to find in stores.
- Subscriptions are a timesaving, hassle-free service.

WHAT ARE THE DISADVANTAGES?

There are some potential downsides associated with subscriptions, which both sellers and customers should be aware of.

For sellers

- Subscriptions prompt customers to evaluate (or re-evaluate) their purchase every month rather than just when a sales representative calls. (It can also be argued that this is an advantage of subscriptions as companies have the potential to converse with customers every month, rather than on an ad-hoc transactional basis).
- Some subscribers are susceptible to short lifespans if their financial situation changes or they have a bad experience.
- In consumer subscription markets, and with the proliferation of subscription services, there are growing concerns about subscription fatigue, especially when combined with other services with subscription-

like characteristics (for example, utilities, insurance policies).

- The upfront cost of acquisition is high, and there is no guarantee that the customer will stay long enough to recoup those costs. The churn factor for Netflix is 1% per month, Spotify sits at around 5% per month, and other companies are even higher.
- Many larger subscription companies leave money on the table. Any subscription company with tens of thousands of customers that they pigeon-hole into three different price points will leave money on the table.

For customers

- They may feel that subscriptions are a waste of money, especially when wastage creeps in (products paid for but not used).
- They may be required to pay for more than they want to consume.
- They may need to better manage their bank accounts, as different subscriptions charges get deducted from bank accounts on different days (requiring the proactive management of a cash buffer).

THE BUSINESS CASE FOR SUBSCRIPTIONS

The table below demonstrates why Wall Street loves subscription businesses so much. The Price-Earnings (PE) ratios shown compare very favorably with the historical average of 13–15 across S&P 500 companies. Apple has only recently shifted its focus becoming a true subscription business (much of its focus has been on hardware to date), which is why it has a lower PE ratio compared to the other subscription businesses.

Company	Share price	Market capitalization	PE ratio	EPS
Apple	US$197.00	US$929 billion	16.25	12.12
Microsoft	US$119.89	US$920 billion	27.81	4.31
Amazon	US$1,837.28	US$902 billion	91.23	20.14
Netflix	US$365.49	US$160 billion	136.38	2.68
Adobe	US$267.45	US$131 billion	49.62	5.39

Since subscriptions are such a popular and powerful pricing model, let's look at how adopting the subscription model has impacted one of its global market leaders.

CASE STUDY: AMAZON

Amazon qualifies as a subscription company. Its Amazon Prime service has been running for several years. On April 26, 2018, it raised its annual subscription price from US$99 to US$119. In Chapter 19, we talked about the significance of the left digit in price perceptions, but this courageous price rise did not have a negative effect on its market capitalization.

The graph below shows the market capitalization of Amazon since late April 2018. Although it has not maintained the dizzy heights of September 2018, as of April 2019, it was still up 19.6%. This is a substantial gain by any reckoning.

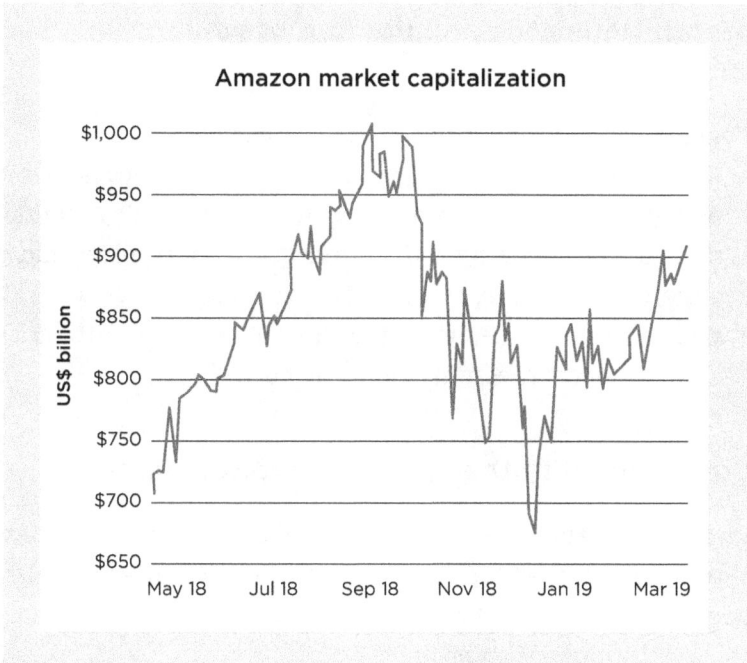

Amazon market capitalization

BUILDING A SUBSCRIPTION PRICING MODEL

Choosing to implement a subscription model is not for the fainthearted. Like any important business process, it requires serious thought and planning as well as collaboration.

Subscription models will be more successful if customers have been involved or consulted as part of the pricing discovery process or the design of the pricing architecture. I have helped many clients develop subscription pricing models using these five simple steps:

Step 1: Define the architecture of your subscription

Consider the architecture of your subscription model:
* How many products do you need in the product ladder?
* Are you going to use a value metric or not? A value metric is a lever by which charges to customers may vary (for example, the number of users).
* Will you offer prices for a month-to-month commitment, a twelve-month commitment, or both?

Step 2: Identify the operative product features

Identify all the operative features of the product that actually do something for the customer. For example, the operative features of practice management software for the legal industry could include:
* customer relationship management
* legal matter management
* workflow automation
* time recording
* expense tracking.

Step 3: Identify the non-operative product features

Identify the non-operative features of the product. These are features that don't affect the operation of the product but do create the ability to further differentiate the architecture. Examples include:
* terms and conditions (for example, payment options, cancellations and refunds, upgrades and downgrades)
* support (for example, account management and

training)
* customization and personalization
* timings (for example, urgent vs standard delivery times, and turnaround times on support requests).

Step 4: Identify optional extras that can be monetized

There are three simple tests to identify an optional extra, which is usually an additional functional feature:
* It doesn't necessarily have to be purchased with the core product offering.
* It can only be consumed after the core product offering has been purchased.
* It can be added to more than one product.
  Examples of optional extras are:
* additional users
* high-definition video
* API integrations for workflow software
* priority support.

Steps 2 to 4 above are represented in the first graphic on the following page, while the second graphic provides an illustrative example of how to design product and pricing architecture for three different types of speaking engagements.

Step 5: Segmentation, value, and willingness to pay

By their nature, many subscription products appeal to a wide audience and are offered at different price points. Prior to launch, you should be prepared to segment your customers according to their economic value, commitment to your product, and willingness to pay.

Add-ons or optional extras
Things that add differentiation
to the options created:
• can buy it now or later
• consumers with a core product/
  not useful on its own
• can be added to more than one product

Non-operative features
Things that add differentiation to the
options created:
• payment terms
• forms of payment
• cancellation fees

Create versions via
Things that add
differentiation to the
options created:
• inclusion or exclusion
• talent or people
• technology
• customization
• timing
• terms and conditions
• education and training
• support
• content

Operative product features
Something you want to
specifically charge for, or bundle
in a specific charge, and three
versions of it can be created:
• customer relationship
  management
• legal matter management
• workflow automation
• time recording

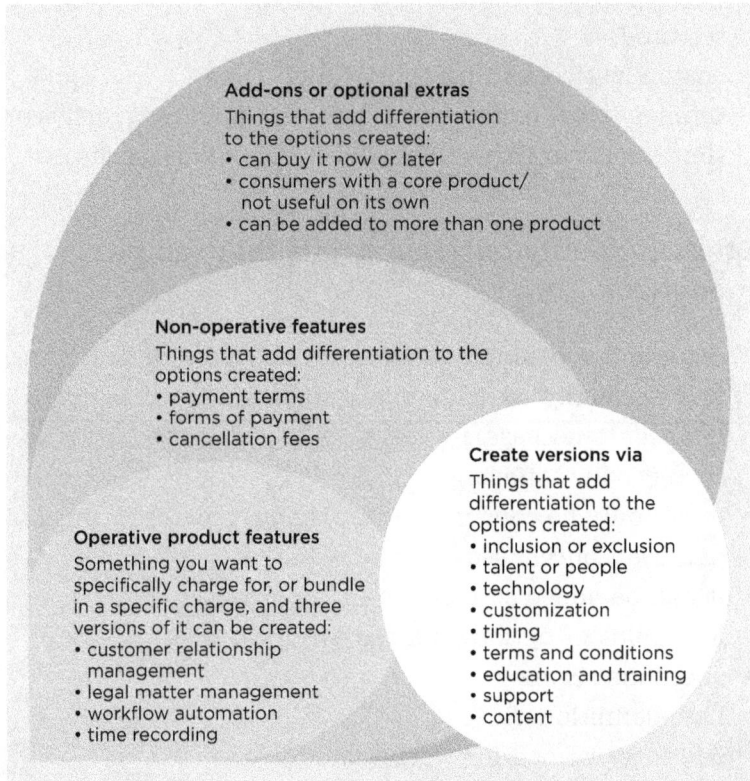

Last, but not least, you should think about the names of the subscription plans. Many businesses name their plans Bronze, Silver, and Gold, or Basic, Intermediate, and Advanced. These names will mean something to their customers, but there are better alternatives. You'll never stand out from the crowd with names like Bronze, Silver and Gold, which – let's face it – really should only be used by businesses in the sports industry.

StewArt Media, a digital marketing agency in Melbourne, had digital marketing subscription packages with some of the best names going around, including Sprinkler, Firehose, Floodgates, and Noah. You can tell what you're going to get just from the names.

$$\text{Product feature} \div \text{Differentiator} = X_1 \ X_2 \ X_3$$

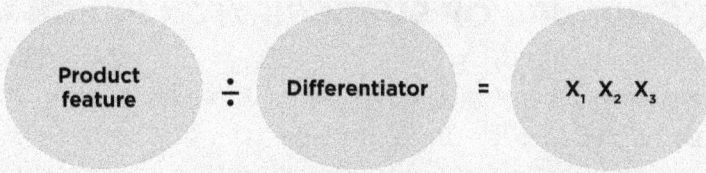

Product feature	Differentiated by	Full-day workshop	Half-day workshop	One-hour keynote
Preparation of material	–	Included	Included	Included
Provision of material (electronically)	–	Included	Included	Included
Delivery of workshop/ keynote	–	Included	Included	Included
Assistance with brochures	Inclusion/ exclusion	Proofreading & feedback on your draft only		Not included
Sales call, pre-sales canvass	Inclusion/ duration	Yes	1 hr (max.)	Not available
Email enquiries answered	Time	24 hrs (max.)	48 hrs (max.)	72 hrs (max.)
Content	Modules	7	4	1
Cancellation penalty	% of investment	20%	30%	50%
Payment due on signing	% of investment	0%	25%	40%
Your investment	–	$US9,500	$US7,250	$US4,800
		Travel & accommodation etc.		

THE FUTURE OF SUBSCRIPTION PRICING

Right now, subscription business models are thriving. Will that be the case in three, five, or 10 years? I have two concerns: one on the business side and the other on the customer side.

From a seller's perspective, subscriptions tick a lot of boxes. But when subscription business scale and have thousands of customers, they will leave money on the table. The more customers a subscription business has, the more money will be left on the table as all those customers are pigeonholed into three plans (Good, Better, and Best, or Bronze, Silver, and Gold). Some of those customers will be prepared to pay more but won't be able to because of the pricing architecture.

From the customer's perspective, there is anecdotal evidence that subscription fatigue is emerging. People are saying they have too many subscriptions. Do they really need Netflix, Stan, Kayo, Disney, Apple, and Amazon Prime?

In business markets, the evidence is more tangible. The existence of platforms that help you manage all your subscriptions and identify what's working and not working for your business confirms this. Ironically, these subscription management platforms offer their services on a subscription basis.

CHAPTER 25

CONCLUSION

"The most important business lesson
I learned in starting my fashion label
was getting my pricing right. There
were plenty of people able to provide
guidance on business plans, public
relations, and the like, but no one would
help me with, or correct, my pricing.
All I wanted to know was that
I wasn't 'shooting in the dark.'"

Kelly Goss, The Bottom Line podcast,
BBC News, 2012

I hope you've gained some knowledge and understanding about pricing and value over the course of this book. Hopefully, I've been able to dispel some of the secrets and mysteries associated with pricing, enabling you to unlock a sustainable, value-based approach to the monetization of your product or service.

One of the reasons it is so difficult to get your head around pricing is because people are so secretive about price and how they arrived at their pricing. As I've said throughout the book, there is no such thing as the perfect price, so you can stop searching for that right now. However, that certainly doesn't mean that understanding pricing is unimportant, and it doesn't explain why people are so unwilling to share information.

CASE STUDY: FLO CAR SHARE

In the early 2000s, while visiting Boston, Monique Conheady discovered the concept of 'car sharing,' which allowed individuals to rent cars by the hour. When she returned to Melbourne's congested roads, she knew that this was a workable idea. By 2004, with the help of some university friends, she had founded Flo Car Share.

By 2006, the business had 1,000 customers around

Melbourne, but Monique had come to the conclusion she had launched the business with the wrong pricing model.

Flo Car Share customers paid a refundable deposit, and then paid by the hour when they used the cars. As long as the car was sitting in a parking spot, waiting for its next booking, expenses like insurance were not being covered. And while, as this book has advocated, you shouldn't price on the basis of cost, you should measure the effectiveness of your pricing by your profitability.

We started by conducting an international benchmarking exercise on the industry and its pricing models. Next we completed an analysis of customer usage and spend, prior to developing new pricing plans along with an estimation of take-up and attrition rates under the new plans. Finally, we developed and implemented communication and migration plans for three consumer and three business market segments.

That communication plan involved telling all customers that Flo had launched with the wrong pricing model. They thought they were providing value to customers, and hoped customers would accept the new pricing model (a monthly subscription fee, accompanied with lower per-hour prices), but they understood if customers wanted to go elsewhere.

It is fair to say that not everything went exactly to plan. There was some customer resistance to the conversion of a prepaid security deposit into the new monthly fee (until the deposit was subsumed).

This would help strengthen Flo's balance sheet, as a contingent liability was converted to revenue.

The fact that Flo, now known as Flexicar (now under the ownership of Hertz), went from strength to strength is testimony to the importance of having the right appetite and attitude toward change and risk.

EXECUTING PRICE CHANGES

Executing any price change isn't easy, and a pricing model change is even harder. Here is a list of suggestions that can help you position a price change/increase.

While explaining the rationale for the price change can be useful, customers care more about the value you provide them than your costs. Remind them what you've done for them recently:

- Remember how well we have supported you in the past?
- We do more than just sell the product/service.
- We search high and low for the best range of products.
- We have over X years of experience in this industry.
- We have world-class showrooms, factories, warehouses, training facilities, support and logistics networks across the country to support our customers.
- We have ISO9001 quality assurance certification.
- We have modern IT capabilities.

It may also be important to point out that this is not an across-the-board money grab. You are using laser-guided missiles, not carpet bombs – changing prices only when you need to. There is certainly no exploitation of market power. In fact, you might even be absorbing a large part of this price increase yourself. It can also be advantageous, especially in highly competitive industries, to announce the change in advance.

Your discussions with customers should be a negotiation, not a surrender. What can you negotiate on? Start with product features, terms and conditions and resort to negotiating on price last. Here are some suggestions:

- If you give me a larger order, I can lower the price.
- Let me pick the color/model/variety for you, and I'll give you a lower price.
- The earlier you give me your order, the lower the price.
- If you can accept a later/less urgent delivery, I can lower the price for you.
- If you pay via cash, I can lower the price.
- If you pay quicker (e.g. 7 days rather than 21), I can lower the price.
- If you also buy X & Y, I can lower the price.
- I can do product X at that price, but not product Y.

Finally, you might want to mention that the price change is temporary. You may reduce prices when interest or exchange rate pressures dissipate.

MANAGING PRICE OBJECTIONS

The customer is the single point of failure in any price change. Executing and making a price change stick may rest, in whole or in part, on your ability to manage customers' expectations and pricing objections. Here are some suggestion to help with that:

- Always time-box the validity of your prices, whether on a proposal or a website, with hard start and end dates.

This applies to both 'list' prices, as well as promotional prices (for example, "Prices apply between 01/12/2019 and 31/06/2020").

- Always present the most expensive option first. If it is one of three options, everything else will be cheaper. But if you present the cheapest first, all the other prices will be more expensive.
- If discussions move into a negotiation phase, ensure those talks take place between equals – in both number and position.
- Keep the focus of the discussion on the smallest number possible. The bigger the number, the more sensitive the customer will be to it. If your price is $20,000 and the customer indicates they're prepared to pay $17,500, focus the discussion on an even smaller number, the $2,500 difference. Similarly, if you're talking about a multi-year contract, focus on the price per annum or, better still, the price per month.

All customers usually have a price they are willing to pay. The last thing you should do is assume a customer is only willing to pay the price you are willing to pay. In such cases, you'll be negotiating with yourself, as well as your customer.

The language and vocabulary used in pricing can also be of critical importance:

- Start by not using the "F word" (that's "fee," not "floccinaucinihiliphication"), which is quite a short, sharp, and harsh word. More preferable alternatives are "investment" or simply "price" instead.
- Likewise, "contract" is a word that many customers can find intimidating and one-way. "Agreement" is seen as more unilateral and accommodating of both sides.
- Finally, avoid using phrases like "This is our normal

price," "This is our regular price," or "This is our standard price." The immediate response to that is going to be "Oh well, there must be a better price then. Let me have it."

It is important to remember that you always want one or two customers complaining about prices. Customers will always tell you that you are too expensive, but they will rarely, if ever, tell you that you are too cheap. Interpret price objections as a sign that a customer is interested in doing business with you.

I once had a head of procurement attend one of my pricing workshops. When I asked why he was there, his reply was simple. "I am here to find out how you people develop pricing and value strategies, so my procurement people can counteract them." (Tip: If you find yourself constantly bumping into procurement managers when selling your product, I'd recommend the reverse: get along to a procurement workshop.)

I asked him if he would tell us some of the tactics in his playbook. These included:

- He always told prospective suppliers, "Your price is just way too expensive" or "You are 16% too high to get this business." This is a sign you've failed to show enough value to substantiate the price you want to charge.
- He always told prospective suppliers, "Price is our only consideration." The reality is that customers like that are more loyal to the cheapest price, whoever they can get that from (not any one supplier).
- He often told prospective suppliers, "Switching to another supplier doesn't cost us anything." The reality is, that's rarely the case. There are costs associated with administration, time, and effort, plus there are psychological, emotional, and social costs.

Three other strategies that have served me well over the years include:

- Firstly, don't start pricing discussions until you know exactly what the customer wants to buy. You wouldn't give the customer a price for Coca-Cola without knowing whether they wanted a can, a bottle, a multi-pack, or an ongoing subscription to kegs for their pub, right? You have to know what the product is before you can price it.
- Secondly, draw comparisons that are meaningful and relevant to the customers. If you are selling parts to an automotive marque, let them know your high-quality parts are highly suited to vehicles like yours, that command exceptionally high prices, and that discerning customers won't be satisfied with a less expensive product.
- And finally, if the negotiation is heading for stalemate and it looks like you'll have to surrender, state that you "need to run that price past my pricing manager" – the CFO or CEO will also do.

PRICING MAY BE YOUR MISSING LINK

Like Monique Conheady of Flo Car Share, you may know that you need to talk to a pricing consultant but are struggling to find one. It's a profession which, if you subscribe to the "bingo and voodoo, invisible hand" school of thought, you probably never knew existed.

No two companies' pricing needs are the same. Regardless of whether they are start-ups or mature business, all companies have different cost structures, different products, and different competitors. Their pricing models can and should be different. This book provides the principles you should follow and outlines a method for thinking and working through. And, while there is no such thing as the perfect price, pricing doesn't have to be a stab in the dark either.

I hope I have left you with a solution to overcoming floccinaucinihilipilification, enabling yourself to value your products and services in a structured and customer-centric way.

I'll close with a quotation from Maureen Wheeler, co-founder of travel guide publisher, Lonely Planet. When asked what she would do differently if she was starting Lonely Planet today, she replied, "I would seek advice from a pricing consultant from the outset."

www.ingramcontent.com/pod-product-compliance
Lightning Source LLC
Chambersburg PA
CBHW032138020426
42334CB00016B/1215